PRAISE FOR

Crossing the Divide: Learning to Love in North Korea

Joy and Stephen are incarnational servants. They humbled themselves to enter North Korea with God's heart and are learning to see the people there through God's eyes. This book is their testimony to the truth that God has never left His people there and that His light continues to shine in the darkness. Clearly, it is a book that God has led them to write at such a time as this. I have admired them for their many years of giving themselves wholly to God's people in North Korea. Everyone who reads this wonderful testimony will see in a new way the great need for reconciliation on the Korean Peninsula and the great need for servants who will minister there. Joy reveals their heart best in her poem, "Why am I here, Lord?" which reads, "I am here for you, Lord. For you—and for you alone." You will be greatly challenged by this book.

DAVID E. ROSS,
Youth With A Mission

Joy and Stephen Yoon have been such an inspiration and treasure trove of insight and information on ministry in North Korea. They have also given an intimate insight into the heart of North Koreans. I always look forward to anything they have to say or write about North Korea. I have always been particularly interested in North Korea because my father and his family escaped from North Korea just before the Korean War began. This new book gives me hope and inspires me to pray for the continued work of the Holy Spirit in North Korea. I look forward to seeing how this book will inspire and impact the future of God's work in North Korea.

JAMES KIM,
Pastor of The Well Church, Gardena, CA

If you are looking for a book that not only talks about loving enemies but also shows what that looks like embodied in daily life, pick up this book. Joy and Stephen Yoon invite us into one of the most closed and misunderstood countries in the world and help us see ordinary people of North Korea wrestle with trauma, resilience, courage, hope, fear, and love—much like the rest of us. Their stories reveal mutual transformation that gives us hope that peace and reconciliation are within reach and that loving our enemies is our blessed work together.

SUE PARK-HUR,
Founder of ReconciliAsian

With grace and honesty, Joy and Stephen Yoon's *Crossing the Divide: Learning to Love in North Korea* opens a window into their difficult but fruitful journey of faith and obedience while living among North Koreans. Together with their team, their work has impacted many lives in deeply profound ways. The richness of this book lies in the illumination of how walking the way of the cross— marked by struggle and challenge, disappointment and hardship, confusion and faith, provision and joy—has transformed their lives, family, outlook, and relationships while opening pathways into the hearts and lives of North Koreans. May this book inspire others to follow their example for the glory of God.

HEIDI LINTON,
Executive Director of Christian Friends of Korea

Do yourself a favor and read this book about living, working, and loving the people in North Korea. It is radical. It is authentic. It is painful yet hopeful. Joy and Stephen Yoon, along with their children, take us on their personal journey in North Korea, telling their stories of how they learned to love as Christ would love, especially children with disabilities. The Yoons enrich our understanding of North Korea. Their vulnerability in revealing their struggles, fears, and desires as ordinary people trusting in God gives us all encouragement to go and do likewise, wherever we live.

BEN AND LIZ TORREY,
The Fourth River Project at Jesus Abbey's Three Seas Center

Joy and Stephen Yoon and their children did what seemed impossible: they lived and worked with North Koreans for years, both in the remote northeastern part of North Korea and in Pyongyang. In *Crossing the Divide: Learning to Love in North Korea*, the Yoons reveal North Koreans for who they really are: broken and beautiful human beings created in the image of God, just as we are. Through acts of profound compassion, perseverance, and courage, the Yoons and their North Korean colleagues have changed the lives of children with disabilities across North Korea. I highly recommend this book.

RANDALL SPADONI,
former Program Director of World Vision North Korea

Joy and Stephen take you on an incredible journey—one guided by faith and hope—where they transform the lives of North Koreans while being forever changed themselves. *Crossing the Divide: Learning to Love in North Korea* is a must-read for anyone who wants to truly understand the most enigmatic country in the world.

CHRISTINE AHN,

CEO of Women Cross DMZ

The Yoons' story explodes a reader's casual interest with God into technicolor awe. God still calls and equips us to do the impossible, still opens doors of opportunity, and still sends us accomplices we never even recruited. These pages don't merely explain how 16 schools, an unlikely medical practice in the North Korean capital, and miraculous education therapies for disabled children emerged out of nothing. They also motivate. You will finish this book more ready for your own step of faith.

GREGG CHENOWETH,

President of Olivet Nazarene University (ONU)

One of the many things I love about Joy and Stephen Yoon is their deep commitment to following God's call regardless of the difficulties or the seeming impossibilities in the face of challenges. In *Crossing the Divide: Learning to Love in North Korea*, they share their story in a compelling and inspiring way that will remind you that nothing is impossible with God and that every person is valuable.

MATT MIKALATOS,

Author of Journey to Love

Crossing the Divide is an uncommon adventure in discovering faith and love in North Korea. Stephen and Joy's realistic account of their struggles and triumphs living north of the 38th parallel invites us to join them in a lifestyle of reconciliation and personal sacrifice that requires unfailing trust in the God whose love knows no boundaries. For those who follow God's clear command to love others, this book is a must-read.

JOHN C. JORDAN,
Associate Lead Pastor, Village Church, Beaverton, Oregon

CROSSING
THE DIVIDE

LEARNING TO LOVE
IN NORTH KOREA

STEPHEN AND JOY YOON

PRESS

Published by StoryBuilders Press

Paperback: 978-1-954521-43-8
eBook: 978-1-954521-44-5

This book is dedicated to the children with disabilities all around the world, to their families, and to the precious sanctity and value of their lives, as they embody God's unconditional love to a broken world.

CONTENTS

Prologue 1

1. A Leap of Faith.. 3
2. The Night God Called Me 9
3. Studying Hard, Trusting Harder 15
4. God Makes a Way 24
5. Unexpected Provision... 30
6. Stepping into the Unknown.. 35
7. Danger and Opportunity.. 41
8. Don't Walk Alone... 48
9. Seeing Their Humanity 55
10. Not According to Our Plans but According to Their Needs 61
11. Love Is Just Love.. 66
12. The Paradox of Empty Pockets....................................... 70
13. Building a Foundation of Love.. 76
14. By This, They'll Know You're My Disciples 80
15. It Never Goes as Planned 87
16. Relational Breakthroughs 93
17. Unity through Difficulty 98
18. God Is Alive in North Korea 103
19. Declaring His Praise 109
20. Raised Up 112
21. Ordained Opportunity..119
22. Immanuel, God with Us 125
23. The Real Battle 129
24. Learning to Love Each Other 134

25. The Gift of Blessing 139

26. When Children Can Dream 145

27. Enlarging our Vision.. 150

28. Building Hope for Children............................... 154

29. Called, Not Qualified...161

30. Love Meets You Where You Are 166

31. When the Harvest Is Hidden...............................171

32. Financial Support Isn't Just about Money 175

33. Special Gifts for Our Family............................. 181

34. Living as Worshipers.. 188

35. Earning Respect by Sharing the Struggle 196

36. Divisions at Home 204

37. Why Am I Here, Lord? 212

38. Living Incarnationally 217

39. Our Task of Reconciliation 222

40. Seeing North Korea Through God's Eyes 227

Support the IGNIS Community................................... 232

Acknowledgments 233

About the Authors 234

PROLOGUE

One day, we visited a well-respected professor. When we departed from the meeting, the professor—with tears in his eyes—prayed that we might become people who disappear quietly like the morning dew. Since then, we've been wondering what it means to live like the morning dew—that is, to be a still drop of water that evaporates soon after creating a beautiful reflection of light.

In *Crossing the Divide: Learning to Love in North Korea*, we share honestly about the heart of Christ that we experienced while living as Christians in North Korea. It's a collection of stories from our everyday lives that offers a unique yet serious glimpse into our time in North Korea, and we dedicate this book to children with disabilities, their parents and caregivers, and the medical professionals who care for them.

We decided to pen our stories because of the first pediatric patient with quadriplegic cerebral palsy whom we treated in North Korea. (Read more in Chapter 25: "The Gift of Blessing.") This little girl, whom we nicknamed Blessing, taught our family about love and gave us motivation to get through difficult times. She is no longer with us but remains God's unexpected gift to our family. We want to tell the world about her and offer glimpses into our daily struggles in saving lives in North Korea.

This book is by no means only about us and our family. It is about our Christian non-profit organization (NGO) called IGNIS Community, also known as Sunyang Hana in Korean. IGNIS Community is a fellowship of brothers and sisters in Christ who have dedicated their lives to cross the divide and venture into those hard-to-reach places where others are reluctant to go. The stories in this book depict how they have made their way into North Korea as ambassadors of love.

Learning to Love in North Korea is a message of reconciliation, love, and service made possible by our supporters and donors from all around the world, who have been praying for our family and for IGNIS Community. We pray that our stories will reflect the light and goodness of Christ, who loves and cares for all people, including North Koreans.

Lastly, we would like to express our deep gratitude and respect to all who have given life to our stories of reconciliation. May we resemble those drops of morning dew at dawn. We pray that what remains in your memory is not us, our names, or what we have done but rather the beauty, grace, and power of our Savior's love.

J O Y A N D S T E P H E N Y O O N

A LEAP OF FAITH

J O Y

We live by faith, not by sight.

—2 CORINTHIANS 5:7

In a satellite image of Earth, North Korea appears only as a dark void between China and South Korea. South Korea shines bright with electricity while North Korea is predominantly pitch-black. Hardly a single light emits from that land.

That's pretty much all we knew of North Korea. We thought of it as the place where people went to be imprisoned, even tortured and killed.

Labor camps. Communist dictatorship. Robotlike control. Missile tests. That's probably what you think of when you think of North Korea too.

At the end of World War II, the fate of Korea was decided by foreign powers without the consultation of the Korean people themselves. The Yalta Conference in February 1945 determined that the Soviet Union would enter from the north when Korea was liberated from Japan to ensure their involvement in World War II. However, this decision coincided with the onset of the Cold War. As a result, when the Soviet troops entered from the north and the US troops from the south to liberate Korea from Japanese occupation, they met in the middle of the peninsula along the 38th parallel. Instead of working together to establish a unified Korea, the two superpowers clashed, setting the stage for the Korean War and the division of the nation. This demarcation line along the 38th parallel became the border between the communist North and the democratic South, a division that continues to this day.

Ironically, what was meant to be liberation set the stage for more than seventy years of conflict.

At the forefront of the Cold War, communism was established in the North and democracy in the South. These two opposing ideologies clashed and resulted in the Korean War. It lasted only three years but killed 3–5 million people. With the peninsula in ruins, a ceasefire was signed between the joint US and UN troops and the North Korean army on July 27, 1953. But a peace treaty has never been established. For over seventy years, North Korea has maintained a totalitarian communist regime.

Maybe you're thinking we'd taken a huge leap of faith to travel there and that we must be out of our minds to have moved there. Maybe we had. Maybe we were. But what we found was that North Korea is perhaps one of the most misunderstood nations in the world. It is dark, but once we experienced the reality of North Korea, we saw it was nothing like what we expected. A curtain was pulled back to a world we did not know existed. Our lives were forever changed.

In April 2007, the two of us sat in the border checkpoint building along the border between China and North Korea, chilled almost to the bone. It was technically spring, but there was no heat, and the outside and inside temperatures hovered just above freezing. Hot-water pipes were cold to the touch and resonated an empty, hollow echo when knocked on.

Most hotel heating in Korea is electric, and most electricity in North Korea comes from hydropower due to sanctions on building alternative power plants. In the winter, the water freezes, and generating energy from it becomes impossible. In the spring, as the water begins to thaw and flow, both are diverted to the farms to facilitate the spring planting. In order to conserve power, electricity is only run for about two hours each day. That makes the twenty-two remaining hours in the day extremely cold. Temperatures in the North can drop down as low as -4°F to -20°F. We would come to know this cold and lack of water well.

A few hours passed before the immigration officers returned from their lunch break. Men in full green military uniforms resumed their official positions, and we were asked to step through the metal detector. An immigration officer scanned our foreheads.

What is this? I thought. *Scanning for microchips?* But no, it was just a thermometer checking for fever.

Once through customs and immigration, the tension in our shoulders and neck relaxed a little, and the ride into town was magical. Despite the bumps and jolts from the rocky mountain terrain, the car was warmer than the station had been, and the scenery was exquisite. Dark-green pine trees canopied the steep mountainsides. Houses with whitewashed walls and drab red-shingled roofs were scattered on the roadside, surrounded by gardens with wooden picket fences. Pink and purple cosmos flowers lined the dirt road parallel to adjacent flooded rice paddies. Young children with red scarves around their necks and backpacks on their backs walked to their small village school. A farmer with an ox and cart plodded his way to the fields. My eyes remained glued to the window as I took in this traditional, magical Asian landscape.

We could see the small city sprawled before us as we approached from the top of the last hill. One truck passed us heading out of the city, its back loaded to the brim with people. Women wore scarves over their heads to protect themselves from the cold and wind. There was a drastic lack of color to them, but the buildings were clean and well kept though drab.

The people too were mostly dressed in typical North Korean clothing, similar to a Chinese Mao suit, wearing one of three solid colors: black, gray, or brown. But they were beautiful with their black hair pulled back sleekly by plastic barrettes. I was surprised to see that most women wore makeup: light-skinned foundation with eyebrow liner and bright red lipstick. Waitresses in restaurants wore surprisingly brightly colored business-type dress suits. Men were thin, but their strength was apparent in their toned arms and muscles and their ability to carry heavy loads on their backs.

As we stepped inside the city's immigration office to register our arrival in the city, my arm brushed up against the wall, and the paint flaked off and onto my jacket. Furniture was arranged in a very formal setting: desks for the office and sofa chairs with coffee tables facing in one direction. Doilies covered both the head and arms of the sofa chairs. The arrangement was not for comfort or conversation but for business.

Once past the initial formal introductions and familiarities, people were kindhearted and generous. They were almost innocent, unpolluted by pop culture and materialism. It felt like we had stepped back into a simpler time, frozen in time to the era just after the Korean War in the 1950s.

Most Americans today can no longer travel to North Korea. Travel restrictions only allow exemptions for humanitarian workers, reporters, and a few other specific purposes in the interest of the US government.

So we want to invite you on a once-in-a-lifetime trip deep into the country of North Korea. Through our story, we will pull back the mysterious shroud hovering over her land and people. We will shine light for you where there is darkness.

You may feel at first like you are stepping into enemy territory. That's also how we felt on this cold day in April. But also, like us, you will slowly, step by step, become more comfortable and at home with the people of North Korea.

Perhaps your world too will be flipped upside down.

As you read through our personal, true stories, a different, truer version of "North Korea" will bloom.

You will begin to see that dark places don't just reside "over there" but there may be some dark places in your own life as well. Perhaps there is a person or relationship that seems impossible for you to relate to. Perhaps you feel the heavy weight of conflict and polarization in your family, church, or community. What boundaries might you need to cross to see them in a completely new light?

We are thrilled you're on this journey with us. Just like taking any short-term mission trip, you first need to get to know your team. That's me, Joy, and my husband, Stephen, and our growing family. We are your crazy new teammates—crazy enough not only to move to North Korea but also to choose to raise our children there.

In the coming chapters, you'll learn what compelled us to go, what propels us to stay, and how we've learned that the Light that exists in North Korea is the same Light that exists where you live, work, and worship as well.

THE NIGHT
GOD CALLED ME

STEPHEN

*But God chose the foolish things of the world
to shame the wise; God chose the weak
things of the world to shame the strong.*

—1 CORINTHIANS 1:27

I began swimming in the fourth grade. Entering middle school as an athlete, I was selected to join the junior national water polo team and enjoyed the full benefits of being a star athlete. But athletics was never my aspiration. I was pushed into sports because of being blocked in other ways. Swimming was plan B. On the surface, it might have appeared as though I had a privileged athletic life, but I actually had concerns throughout my school days that I hid behind the scenes.

My secret was a deep sense of inferiority.

As in most Korean homes and as the eldest son in my family, I was destined for a specific trajectory—specifically, academic success that would lead to a career as a lawyer, doctor, or other highly respected professional.

There was one problem.

I made poor grades in school. Whenever I took exams, I would still be working hard when the bell rang. I was never able to complete the test questions on time. Reading was slow and difficult. I didn't know it at the time, but I was dyslexic. I always thought I just lagged behind others and was not smart. Years later, as I began treating children with disabilities, I realized that I had a reading disability. Even today I am slow at reading. My own lectures are difficult for me to read.

It is absurd that I became a doctor, but that's how the grace of God works sometimes.

My mother was passionate about my education and employed a tutor from the Department of Mathematics at Seoul National University to help me improve. Surprisingly, after being tutored, for the first time in my life, I was able to solve all the math problems on my test. I ran home and triumphantly boasted to my mother that I thought that I had finally scored a perfect grade on my exam. My mother congratulated me by preparing my favorite food. However, a few days later, when I returned to class, I found all the test papers graded and lying on each student's desk. Every student had received their test score except for me. I thought that was strange, so I looked inside my desk, and my test paper was there. With great anticipation, I took out my exam, but when I finally looked at my score, I could not believe my eyes. I had received a zero! Not a single problem was correct.

For the first time in my life, I was able to solve all the problems, I thought, and I expected to get a perfect score. I could not believe it! *What happened?* I wondered.

When I think about it now, I think the teacher was extremely gracious by protecting me from humiliation by putting my test paper inside my desk.

My mother wasn't quite so gentle and could not accept my failing grade. I remember being spanked to a pulp that day. Shocked by my performance, my mother decided my academic career was over and instead sent me to begin swimming lessons.

Although I was only an elementary school student, I was so fat that my waist was as wide as an average adult's. Instead of starting with the freestyle stroke, I started learning the backstroke. Since most young swimmers start competing in freestyle, there were few other athletes in my age bracket competing in backstroke.

I spent my middle school and high school years in boarding school and focused on my athletics. At competitions, I usually ended up winning second or third place. As someone who was always the lowest-ranked student in class, winning prizes in front of my classmates was a great motivation for me to keep swimming.

However, there were still days, even as a successful athlete, when I was depressed because of my lack of academic success. I was confident in my intelligence, but I could not adequately demonstrate it in my schoolwork. This not only frustrated me, but I also often felt defeated by it.

This was true even as I entered college. Even in my twenties, as a college student who participated in international sports competitions on the national team, I *still* could not read my textbooks well due to my dyslexia, and it really did a number on my self-esteem.

The only thing I believed I knew how to do well was swim.

This filled me with shame and an inferiority complex.

As a result, I became timid, afraid that others might find out who I *really* was.

Although I was from the city of Incheon, I moved to Seoul in 1986 as a national athlete and began attending the Church for Athletes. There I dived headfirst into my faith.

One night an unforgettable event occurred. A meeting was held as part of the Sports Fellowship. A large number of people attended, and at the end of the sermon, the pastor asked a question to the congregation.

"If God asks you to go to a country that is far away, would you say yes? If you would like to say yes, come forward."

Our pastor was nurturing us with the vision for elite athletes to reach countries all around the world. That night the pastor's challenge moved my heart. In my mind, everyone ought to say yes to his question. His question simply indicated that Christians should live a life of sharing God's love through their talents wherever they go.

I responded without thinking.

I jumped up and walked forward. I felt a little awkward, and when I turned around, no one else was following me down the aisle. I had expected everyone in the room to get up. But my friends just sat there staring at me with worried eyes. We exchanged silent glances. Everyone was looking at me, but at that point, it was impossible for me to turn back. My choice had already been made. When I finally got down to the altar, the pastor laid his hands on my head and prayed over me.

In that moment, something amazing happened. I experienced the overwhelming presence of the Holy Spirit. It was at that moment I realized that God is truly alive, and I dedicated my life to journey with Him for as long as I lived.

Perhaps that was the moment my life truly began. Looking back now, I can recognize that my steps down that aisle were a response to God's definite call upon my life. God called me, full of my feelings of inferiority, just like Jesus had called Zacchaeus who climbed the sycamore tree.

My calling did not start with my determined aspirations.

God didn't look at my talents or abilities.

He just looked at the heart of one who would obey His Word. When I thought I had nothing to offer, God chose me, crippled in shame, and asked me to share His love with this world. As the scripture says, "He chose the foolish things of the world to shame the wise, and chose the weak things of the world to shame the strong" (1 Corinthians 1:27).

God called me in my weakness. Little did I know then that He would have to make me strong.

God's standards and thoughts are different from our own. It's not about what *you* can offer God—you'll always feel inferior—but rather *who* He is and how He has decided to use you. When we look at ourselves, we often only see our limitations or the bad in us. But when you look to God, there is hope.

That night I had nothing to offer but my humble obedience and my secret inferiority, but God called me just as I was to journey with Him.

This was the greatest blessing of my life.

What is holding you back? If you surrender to Him, He can do the same for you. It was only thanks to my faith that I began to change, little by little.

STUDYING HARD,
TRUSTING HARDER

STEPHEN

*With man this is impossible, but with
God all things are possible.*

—MATTHEW 19:26

Living life means that you must endure the heat and the cold; the joys and the sorrows; the seasonal drifts of spring, summer, autumn, and winter. So it is with faith. To have tasted grace means that hardships have come, and after having endured those trials, you receive a deeper sense of grace.

In our faith journey, we often hear the well-intentioned advice that the greater the suffering, the deeper the experience of God's grace is. That doesn't make it easy to endure the pain that comes before the grace—no matter what kind of suffering it entails. Looking back, I wonder if I was able to endure hardships because God gave me the strength to do so, or if perhaps God only gave me the amount of suffering that I was able to handle.

What is clear is that the providence of God worked all things together for my good.

After that night in church, when I experienced the incredible grace of God, an unexpected time of hardship followed. My mother had been battling lymph cancer, and as the cancer spread throughout her body, she endured even more pain. Organs were removed from her body to prevent the cancer from spreading any further. Seeing my mother succumb to cancer, I could do nothing but pray. A fountain of tears flowed every night as I prayed more earnestly than ever before, depending upon the Lord to heal my mother.

But in the end, my mother died.

Even though I'd spent little time with my mother since elementary school, losing her was indescribable. The void of no longer having my strongest supporter with me seemed too great for me to bear.

I also felt a lot of guilt. In Korean culture, all parents expect that their efforts in raising their children will return to them over time. Children are their parents' retirement investment, and the oldest son is expected to care for his elderly parents as repayment for the care he was provided. Thinking of how much my mother sacrificed and cared for me and knowing that I had done nothing for her in return left me with immense regret.

With nowhere else to turn, I went to God and fell on my face and wept. God came to me, patted me on the back, and quietly wiped away my tears. He comforted me, hugged me, and spoke words of praise to me as my loving Father. The more I felt His warm touch, the closer I came to God and personally knew my living Savior.

As I released my mother to heaven, my faith grew even stronger. Through this time, God was solidly growing my faith in Him. The Lord met me and accepted me, even though I was still battling my sense of inferiority. Despite feeling that I was full of shortcomings, He did not compare me to anyone else. As I simply rested in Him, I became free, just as scripture says that the truth will set you free.

After my mother's death, I wanted to confirm God's calling and vision upon my life. I wanted to do something meaningful, something other than sports. Up until then, I had no other thoughts as to what I could do with my life. One thing I knew—my love and passion for God seemed to be more intense than that of anyone else I knew.

So I decided to lean into that and see what God was up to.

I started specifically asking God what I should do. I asked Him what He wanted from me. One day, while praying, God gave me a heart to "challenge the impossible."

The impossible?

Immediately, my mind flashed back to the zero on my elementary school math exam and how painful that was. As I thought about it, the only impossible thing for me was studying.

I had no doubt that it was God's Word to me, but it seemed out of place. But I didn't ask God why. I knew my job was to obey, not to ask questions. I decided to do the most impossible thing in my life for God—study.

I began to pray more about what kind of study God wanted me to pursue. Since swimming was the only thing that I could do, I first thought I should study physical education. But that brought my heart no peace as I prayed.

I pressed on, continuing to pray until one day, God whispered, *Medicine.*

A doctor?

I was shocked. This was definitely an impossible thing. I gave it a prospect of success of less than one percent. Whatever it was that God was up to, I was up for a challenge. But just to be sure, I prayed again. Perhaps God meant to send that response to the person in the next room, the person who could read well and study hard and make good grades, and the answer to their prayers came to me by mistake.

It was no mistake.

God was asking me to be a doctor. But as I thought more about it, I realized that studying medicine, which was something I would never dare try on my own, was one of *the most impossible things* God could have asked of me.

So if God called me, God would make it happen.

It was His golden opportunity to show His power and ability by choosing me, the weakest of all people.

From that day on, I dreamed of going to America to become a doctor. I had decided to study abroad. When I told my father, Sungsoo Yoon, that I wanted to go to America to study medicine, he was staunchly against it. The first words out of his mouth were, "You are officially crazy."

I can see how this dream must have looked impossible to my father. Put yourself in his position. He'd watched me struggle academically and prioritize athletics instead for many years, and at the time, I could not speak a single word of English. He must have thought that I just wanted to waste his money before eventually coming back home again.

But even I could admit the idea was fairly reckless.

But is recklessness *for God* really all that reckless?

I had no other choice but to hold on to God, who promised to make the impossible possible.

A fellow swimmer friend of mine from Korea lived in Chicago, so I went there and started learning English. My dorm roommate was one of the few Asians on campus, but he happened to be Japanese. Many Americans don't realize that there is often animosity between Japanese and Koreans. To be honest, Koreans often despise the Japanese, but our shared faith and solidarity in our circumstances forged a bond between us despite historical tensions between our nations.

As you can imagine, everything was a challenge. I was able to communicate to some extent, but when I started studying in English, it was very difficult. I had numerous car accidents driving the streets of the city, and I was even robbed at gunpoint in Downtown Chicago because I didn't know which places were safe to go alone.

In order for me to enter an American university as a foreign student, a TOEFL (Test of English as a Foreign Language) score of 500 or more was required at the time. It felt like an impossible obstacle to overcome for me to even go to college, let alone become a doctor.

At that time, my roommate, who was also enrolled in the English learning program, asked me if I could go with him for his interview at the university he was hoping to attend after our program at the University of Illinois at Chicago was finished. I was happy to put down my studies and get out of our dorm, so I joined him for a tour of the school. It was a Christian university called Olivet Nazarene University just south of Chicago.

As I was waiting for my friend in front of the admissions office, I suddenly had a thought that I should apply to the school too. I signed my name on the appointment list to let them know that I was waiting for an interview.

A bit later, a counselor graciously met with me, even though I did not have an appointment, and asked me if there was anything I would like to say. I was nervous, but I managed to calmly tell my story. And even though my TOEFL score was not good, I explained in detail that the reason I had come to the United States was in obedience to God's call upon my life. I displayed a strong will to become a doctor and was more serious and passionate than ever. I reasoned that if a Christian school like this one wouldn't accept me, a man passionate for God, then what kind of school would? In my mind, this school *must* accept me.

I spoke so confidently that I didn't even know where that confidence was coming from.

The counselor admitted me on the spot with a faint smile.

"Really?" I asked, surprised that the door had opened so easily and so soon.

Instead of turning me away, I was offered a conditional acceptance. The counselor informed me that if I received just one failing grade in my first year studying, I would be required to retake the TOEFL and achieve a passing score. Shocked—and not wanting to push my luck any further—I readily replied that I would abide by that promise. It was a miracle that I was accepted to the school my friend was applying to—and even with a TOEFL score of less than 500!

God's guidance in my life was clearly evident.

Since my conditional acceptance was based on passing all my classes, I focused all my attention on studying. When others might have studied for two hours, I studied for eight. Once I sat down to study, it felt like I would never get up. I read slowly because of my dyslexia, and since I had failed my elementary school math exam, I had to start studying arithmetic from basic fractions. I worked hard to catch up on my education—an education I had pretty much missed since primary school. Even though studying felt like a full-time job, I still had to work to pay the bills. I washed dishes in our school cafeteria, worked part-time in our campus boiler room at night, and sold things at a flea market on the weekends. But even with all these part-time jobs, I often studied all night long.

Thanks to the discipline of my intense athletic training, I was able to study hard. Knowing how hard I had pushed myself in athletics, I knew how to push past my limits. Despite the agony, I was grateful for the grueling athletic training that prepared me for this difficult time. God truly does not waste any of our experiences.

As I did my best to keep my promise to the admissions counselor, I graduated from Olivet Nazarene University without receiving a single failing grade after entering my major studies in the biology department.

Through this experience, God changed me.

Ironically, I, who had failed that fourth-grade math test, became a math tutor in the United States. When I shared this news with my father in Korea, he could not believe it. And yet, it was through this excruciating study regime that the inferiority complex I had struggled with my whole life began to disappear.

It's a good thing, because I wasn't done studying.

After my undergraduate studies, I went to Cleveland Chiropractic College in Los Angeles, where I received a doctorate in chiropractic degree. I treat and correct the spine, lower back, and joints by applying adjustment primarily by hand, without any surgical equipment. When I was deciding upon my medical field, many people suggested that I go into surgery or internal medicine. But chiropractic appealed most to me. I had no idea how God would miraculously use this specialty inside of North Korea, but I followed my instinct and desire.

My entire journey has been led by God's hands. Although I felt insufficient in many ways, through my personal encounter with God, I was determined to unconditionally obey Him. Just as the waters split when the priests carried the Ark of the Covenant across the Jordan River in Joshua chapter three, as I obeyed the Word of God and took one step of faith, God made the impossible possible by splitting the waters in front of me.

I had come this far after hearing *just one Word* from the Lord that challenged me to do the impossible. All I had to do was follow His Word, step forward, work with all my might, and hold on to God. It's not always easy, but through obedience, God instilled in me a confidence to follow Him wherever that might lead. He built me up, restored my self-esteem, and healed my sense of inferiority.

What I have realized through my story is that my job is to believe in His Word and take a step forward. God will do the rest. I must give my best and wait for His guidance. I have no power to make the impossible possible. Only God can do that. As I followed Him step by step in faith, the parts of my life that I deemed impossible, God miraculously transformed into the possible.

I would challenge you to do the same thing. Listen for His voice, take a step forward, and lean on His sufficiency to do the impossible through you.

GOD MAKES A WAY

JOY

*Before you were born I set you apart; I
appointed you as a prophet to the nations.*

—JEREMIAH 1:5

I met my husband, Stephen, in the fall of 1995. We were both in
college. He was the only Korean on campus. Although I was
American, we quickly became friends because of our shared connection—we both grew up in Korea. We also both majored in biology and were active in the same international club with similar
interests, so we had many things in common. Our vision was to
serve overseas as Christian professionals. Since we were young
and burning with passion, we had a deep conversation about how
we were going to make all this happen.

At that time, Stephen was interested in the Middle East. He thought this was what God meant by having a heart to go to a faraway and difficult place. I had a different vision: I had a heart for North Korea. While talking, I shared with Stephen how I had developed a special heart for this misunderstood and villainized nation.

I moved with my parents to Korea when I was only two years old. My parents were commissioned as international missionaries by the Church of the Nazarene. My father and mother both served in Daejeon and Cheonan for twenty-five years, teaching students as professors at Korea Nazarene University in Cheonan.

As I grew up in Korea from a tiny toddler until my graduation from high school, I suffered from an identity crisis, similar to how many missionary kids and immigrant children feel. Although I lived much of my life in Korea, I did not feel that Koreans accepted me because I was white. Every four years our family would travel to the United States for a sabbatical year, but I had trouble adapting to American culture and just wanted to return to Korea as soon as possible.

I might have been born in America, but it certainly didn't feel like home to me.

I did not know who I was or where I belonged as I struggled with my identity. I thought that I had no real home. Wherever I went, I felt like a stranger. Living as a typical third-culture kid who moved from city to city, confused about where my roots were between Korean and American cultures, I often saw myself as a boiled egg with contrasting exterior and interior. Although I looked white on the outside, I was more Asian on the inside.

While I was going through this deep anxiety, I attended a conference with my parents and there heard the clear, bright words of the Lord.

Surprisingly, God told me, *Go to North Korea.*

As an American and South Korean resident, North Korea was a mysterious land that necessitated me to practice blackout drills and fear for my safety. However, God had already started to work on my heart. I had done quite a bit of reading about Korean history, including North Korea. So when I first heard God's calling, it all started to make sense to me. Despite my own swirl of cultural confusion, when I heard God's voice, true peace came over me for the first time. I began to understand that God allowed me to grow up in South Korea so that I could serve Him one day in the North.

I was only fifteen years old, but from that moment on, I envisioned North Korea as my home and her people as my people. Hearing God's voice that day, I instantly understood His purpose for having me grow up in South Korea. It was the training ground for my mission.

From that day on, I had a heart for North Korea and dedicated my life to that land. It didn't matter that there was no way to go to North Korea. It didn't matter that the news about North Korea in the 1990s was only about nuclear weapons and famine.

When I committed myself to the Lord to go live in North Korea, *no one* around me believed it could be done. Everyone saw it as just a silly dream of a teenage girl. It didn't matter. *I* began to dream that impossible dream. I did not know when or how I would go, but I knew one day I would be living in North Korea. Even if that moment was not for a long time, I was determined to wait until that dream came true.

People often ask Stephen how he got the idea of going to North Korea. The truth is that his heart for North Korea started with my calling, not his. Unlike me, Stephen had never before thought about North Korea.

In fact, Stephen had never dared to imagine going there because he grew up in South Korea. He had a preconceived (and not at all positive) notion about North Korea.

Around the time we were contemplating marriage, I asked Stephen a life-altering question.

"I know you feel called to Middle Eastern Islamic nations, and I can follow you there, but what would you do if God told our family to live in North Korea?"

His answer didn't take long. "If God tells us to go, we should go."

Later I learned that in those words was Stephen's conviction that God would *never* send our family there. Not knowing this, I heard his answer and decided that he was the man for me. We got married before our senior year in college.

Several years later, in the middle of graduate school, we got a call from a close friend. There was a conference on the theme of North Korea, so he suggested we attend it. This was the first conference of its kind, which aimed to mobilize Christians to pray for and engage with North Korea. God was placing North Korea in the hearts of his people.

Stephen was curious, but since our graduate studies were so demanding, we felt financially burdened. In fact, we had no money because both of us were just poor graduate students. We didn't know how we could afford to go, but our friend said that there were scholarships available. (Later we learned that the "scholarship" was actually provided personally by our friend, knowing our circumstances well. Perhaps his generosity was what brought our family to live in North Korea.)

One day at the conference, an amazing meeting took place. In that meeting, Stephen met a second-generation Korean American family who was living in North Korea doing business. They had been living there for four years with young children. The fact that there were people actually living in North Korea, families even with children, came as a refreshing shock. Up until then, Stephen had thought that a person entering North Korea was impossible. He didn't even consider the possibility of living there together as a family.

When he met this family, his heart raced. At home, he excitedly told me about the conference. I listened and broke into a big smile.

"Honey, our time has come. Let's pack our bags and go."

After the conference, God completely changed Stephen's view of North Korea. Until then, he thought that the only distant place he would go to would be the Middle East. Now he realized that place should be North Korea.

At the same time, he was also worried. The vague fear of North Korea that had been taught since he was a child was still in him. However, we were ready to go wherever God called us to go, and more and more, he believed and agreed that this was God's will for us.

North Korea had captured our imagination.

More than anything else, what penetrated our hearts was love. It was love for the Lord rather than love for North Korea. That love was the key that opened our closed hearts. Looking back, throughout the many decisions and sacrifices we have had to make, this constant love has been the subject of our lives.

That love for a misunderstood country flowed from me first and then on to my husband. Stephen at times felt bad that his American wife loved North Korea so much while he struggled to love his fellow Koreans. Although our beginning was not exactly in unison, I knew that in the end, we would burn with passion together. In particular, North Korea is only thought of as a country in need of humanitarian aid. Everyone knows they benefit from donations of rice and medicine, but why doesn't anyone want to live there? The challenge of living in that nation together with our family touched his heart.

We didn't have any plans of anything special to do there or anything big to accomplish. Just as Christ loved us, all we had to do was simply share the love we had already received from God with them as we lived among them.

We were ready to go behind the lines and see what God had planned.

5

UNEXPECTED PROVISION

STEPHEN

*Go from your country, your people, and your
father's household to the land I will show you.*

—GENESIS 12:1

When we told people that we were going to North Korea, no
one congratulated us.

In fact, everyone around us was against it. North Korea was
our enemy. A communist nation led by generations of dictators.
It was not a place to go as a Christian or as an American.

The two of us were serving second-generation Korean
American students in our church in Los Angeles. Our church
encouraged us as a young couple pursuing ministry, but people
were concerned particularly for our two children, five-year-old

Sarah and two-year-old Caleb. They might not have opposed this if it were just us, adults, who were going, but they worried about us taking our children there. People come to America to give their children opportunities and a brighter future. We were leaving the land of opportunity and restricting our children's futures by taking them into one of the most isolated countries on earth.

Certainly, they also assumed the path ahead of us was full of suffering. I felt sad that everyone was concerned for our family, but I could endure their criticism.

Even more than the opposition from our church community was the dread I felt when I considered how and when to break the news to my father. As the eldest son in a Korean family, I was responsible for taking care of my dad. I couldn't bear to tell him that I was leaving for North Korea. The words just would not come out of my mouth. After procrastinating as much as I could, I finally decided to tell him just before our scheduled departure.

We prepared a delicious meal, hoping that that would ease the bad news. Then we explained our vision to my father, telling him where we had decided to go to work.

"Where?"

"North Korea."

As soon as the words came out of my mouth, mid-meal my father abruptly threw down his spoon and started swearing at me.

"You idiot! That's no place to go! That's where you want to go?"

My father immediately left the table.

The next day my father went to an early-morning prayer meeting at our church for the first time in his life. Up until then, my father only attended church at Christmastime and Easter.

Though he had promised my mother before she passed away that he would go to church regularly, it was because of me that my dad began going to church daily.

His prayer every morning was, "Lord, stop my son from going to North Korea."

For this purpose and this purpose only, he went to church diligently to pray every day for several days.

But prayer changes things, and it especially changes the one doing the praying! After a few weeks, my father came to us and asked if he could come with us to North Korea.

This was an unexpected surprise!

Later my father confessed to us the real reason he decided to go with us was not because his faith had radically changed but because he thought that it would be better for his grandchildren if he went with us to help us.

The heart of our Heavenly Father helped us jump over all the obstacles that lay in our path. I often wonder if God allows us to taste these obstacles—in this case, the obstacle that was my father—to show us the power of His love. God is capable of overcoming any obstacle.

Before leaving for North Korea, I was running a multidisciplinary medical clinic in Los Angeles. The church our family served at took over the clinic and asked me to manage it as the head administrator. I thought the experience would be helpful one day, so I took the position and worked hard.

A year before we left, we did not yet have all our financial support. As a result, I was considering postponing our departure. But the story of Horace Underwood, one of the first missionaries to be sent to Korea, gripped our hearts as we heard new insights of it in a message at another conference on North Korea.

Horace Underwood went to Korea with the Presbyterian Church in the nineteenth century, established schools, and greatly contributed to the medical field at that time. Initially, Underwood was preparing to go to another country, but he did not have the finances to leave. A complete stranger approached him and gave him the funds he needed for his work with the condition that he would go to Korea instead. As a result, not only did he serve the Korean people through numerous ministries, but four generations of Underwoods remained serving in Korea.

As both of us heard this story, we felt like God was talking directly to us. Our job was just to obey. We decided to leave as planned to serve the people in North Korea. My wife was confident that God would provide for us. Soon afterward, the phone rang. It was a deacon from another church whom we had met a month before.

"For some reason, you keep coming to my mind. My company would like to support your family through a small donation every month."

After hanging up, we looked at each other and smiled. God provided precisely the funds that we needed. This was God's final confirmation to us that now was the time to go. I often wonder if God works this way to test or grow our faith. He asks us to step out in obedience first, and then God often provides exactly what we need.

Without a doubt in either of our hearts or minds, we prepared to depart with the confidence that the Lord would take care of all our needs while we were living in North Korea.

With all the loose ends tied and our last remaining task in preparation to leave completed, our life was wrapped up in the United States. We headed to East Asia.

In April 2007, fifteen years after Joy felt the call, we took our first trip to North Korea.

6

STEPPING INTO
THE UNKNOWN

JOY

*The people walking in darkness have seen
a great light; on those living in the land of
deep darkness, a light has dawned.*

—ISAIAH 9:2

When we arrived at the border the first time, Stephen was so nervous about crossing that his whole body stiffened. The thought that we were actually going into North Korea that day started to fill us with butterflies.

Stephen remembered the way North Koreans were portrayed to him in posters as a child in South Korea—literally humanlike beings with horns and tails. In the 1970s and 1980s, most North Koreans were depicted this way in the South. So a subtle fear of North Korea had taken place in his heart without him even knowing it. In addition, no matter how hard he tried to remain calm, anxiety continued to overwhelm him. He later confessed to me that he was even secretly hoping that our car's tire would go flat so that we could not go any further.

I, on the other hand, was ecstatic. Having waited fifteen years since I first felt called to be there, I was elated to finally be stepping foot in the country.

At that time, it took about two or three hours from Yanji, China to arrive at the border of North Korea. Looking at the Tumen River from afar, we saw it was bleak. When we arrived at immigration, it was already lunchtime, and the immigration officers had all gone on a lunch break. There was no waiting room for arrivals, and there were no signs indicating where to go. For some reason, our invitation from the organization we were joining was also not processed correctly, and our local guide had not yet arrived. These invitations and guides are required as part of the communist system, much like how minders are required when visiting the Soviet Union.

We waited for the officials to arrive from lunch, shivering for two hours in an empty room with no heating. We cannot recall if we were trembling from the cold or from nervousness or both.

Two North Korean government officials finally came to process us through immigration, and some members of the team we would be working with in North Korea came and accompanied us across the border. Our guide was a native of North Korea and had a boyishly good-looking appearance. Obviously, I knew North Koreans did not have horns and tails, but I didn't expect them to be so good-looking either. I couldn't help but comment quietly to Stephen, "He's so handsome!"

After completing the immigration process, we got back into our car and drove across the border, down the bumpy mountain road, and into the village. Throughout the ride, the officers assigned to accompany us drilled Stephen with personal questions about him and his family. He was frozen stiff. All Stephen could manage to do was to answer an abrupt yes or no. They were probably just making small talk, but because of Stephen's anxiety and fear, he felt like he was being interrogated. I could sense Stephen's tension and gently tried to ease the atmosphere by placing a comforting hand on his shoulder.

Outside the car, the tranquil scenery of North Korea unfolded. Despite the bumps and jolts from the rocky mountain terrain, the scenery was exquisite. It was a landscape of simple, daily life, just like any other rural village in Korea. It reminded me of the Korea I knew long ago as a child.

As is still the case today, most visits to North Korea are made through people who have business relationships in the country. We received an invitation from Pastor Jae-Yell Kim, a Korean Canadian who had been working in North Korea since the 1990s. He had heard about us from a team member of his whom we had met at a conference. He built and operated three hospitals, including dental, obstetrics, and traditional medical clinics. Pastor Kim contacted us not long after we left the United States. He said that he was running a hospital and asked Stephen to help manage it.

At that time, most foreigners working in North Korea were mainly building kindergartens and daycare centers and providing humanitarian aid or benevolent businesses in various ways. There was a special zone within Rason, in the North Hamgyong Province, designated as the first free economic zone in North Korea, where foreigners were permitted to live and work. Because this area was open to receiving business investments and humanitarian support, it was a favorable place for foreigners and overseas Koreans to establish both themselves and their organizations.

In particular, the free economic zone encouraged overseas Koreans to visit North Korea, and the North Korean Association for Overseas Compatriots allowed overseas Koreans with US and UK passports, like Stephen, to come and work in North Korea.

One company that first invited us to work with them was a fertilizer factory. Although we wondered how we could contribute to a fertilizer plant since I was a biology teacher and Stephen was a medical professor, we reasoned that we could join the team because of our vision to live in North Korea. We had no grand goals or plans. We simply just wanted to live in that country and serve where we could.

But we were grateful that we were given this opportunity by Pastor Kim closer to the field of our expertise. Through his invitation, God opened the doors for us to use our skills and training in the medical field in North Korea.

We stayed in a hotel in the center of town. We were told by those who had been to North Korea that every conversation would be bugged and recorded by the government. But just as we normally did in the States, we worshiped every morning and evening in our hotel room to pray for and bless North Korea.

The presence of our guides, who accompanied us at all times, was strange to me at first. Everything we did in our days was monitored by them and reported to the government. In fact, North Koreans must record all conversations they have with foreigners and submit them to the authorities, which makes most North Koreans reluctant to communicate with outsiders.

However, the people we met in North Korea were kindhearted and generous. We were warmly welcomed by those we met even though we were foreigners. On our first visit to the local market, I tried greeting the local vendors in Korean, and they burst into laughter. Children in the market also looked at me and hid behind their mothers' skirts. They were shocked to see foreign faces. Some looked at me with suspicion, but many others greeted me with a smile.

After these emotional ups and downs, we went back to China after our tour of five days and four nights. On this first trip, everything in North Korea still seemed foreign and unfamiliar.

Over the coming years, our tension was transformed into a great harvest of good experiences with the people living there. The friendly Korean people of the countryside that I remembered as a child from South Korea lived in the North as well.

It was a brief trip, but it changed our hearts and lives forever. Our hearts were opening up to deeply loving the North Korean people.

After that, we began going back and forth between China and North Korea repeatedly until we received a formal residential visa. After seeing the place we had only dreamed of for so long, we decided to move in and live there not just temporarily, but perhaps for the rest of our lives. Even with trepidation, not knowing the future, we knew our lives belonged to God, and He had called us to North Korea to share His love with the people there. If we were in the center of God's will for our lives, we had to trust that we were in the safest place we could be.

7

DANGER AND OPPORTUNITY

JOY

*We also glory in our sufferings, because we
know that suffering produces perseverance;
perseverance, character; and character, hope.*

—ROMANS 5:3-4

The word *crisis* in Chinese is a combination of two characters: *danger* and *opportunity*. This was certainly what it felt like for Stephen and me as we were making our way to the border into China from inside North Korea during our third trip into the country in the fall of 2007.

After our initial visit, we arranged to visit again a few months later in the coming summer. Stephen ended up spending an entire month in North Korea as I continued my Korean language studies and took care of the kids in the South.

Our third visit was in the fall for about four days, as the two of us were helping Pastor Jae-Yell Kim with hospital and kindergarten projects in the Rason area. We did not have much time to make it from this region to the border, which closed at 5:00 p.m. We rushed as fast as we could along the bumpy dirt road on our drive out of town. At a railroad crossing, the road was backed up with cars and was impassable. Trains in North Korea ran on electricity, and the electricity had been cut off. The train was stopped in the middle of our road. In North Korea, when the electricity is off, there is no knowing when it will come back on.

Our only solution seemed to be to turn back, but another car started down a small dirt trail. "Where in the world was it going?" we wondered. About three hundred meters down the path was a small ford in the middle of a stream underneath the railroad bridge. There was just enough space for a car to go through, if it could manage the rocky stream. We followed the unfamiliar car in faith, crossing the stream and arriving just in time before immigration closed.

We knew Pastor Kim was scheduled to come out of North Korea late the following day. We were not alarmed when a day passed and he still had not arrived, but the morning after that, we heard the news that he had been detained. We had only started working in North Korea, so we knew little about what to do in this situation. We also felt uneasy since he was the person who had invited us to work in North Korea, and now he was detained.

We had to somehow find a solution. We went to his home country's embassy pleading for his life. Thankfully, many people joined us in praying for his release. After eighty-five days in a detention facility, Pastor Kim was safely released, but unfortunately, he was banned from entering North Korea again. It was a sad day for our team because he had passionately dedicated himself to the people of North Korea. In addition, this incident left our team in a difficult and chaotic situation. Since our team leader was never able to work in North Korea again, we wondered whether or not we would be able to continue the work ourselves.

The way forward was uncertain and frightening. Our team did not know if or how to continue. It helped me understand a little more about what Jesus's disciples might have felt on the Saturday between his death and resurrection.

Pastor Kim had asked us to take over the work that he had been doing. We had numerous discussions with our team members, but we were all at a crossroads as to whether or not we should continue the ministry or give it up altogether. We worried that our proximity to him might endanger both our safety and hinder our family's dream of living in North Korea. After deep discussion, it became apparent that our purpose was to hold on to the calling of our first love. We were to be in North Korea to show the love of Christ.

We did not have the confidence that we would succeed, as North Korea was still extremely foreign to us, but we knew that nothing could separate us from God's love—neither the fears for today nor our worries about tomorrow (Romans 8:38). We unanimously decided to continue the work.

Pastor Kim reminded us to be an example of God's unconditional love. He confessed to us that even though he had loved North Koreans, he had failed to love all North Koreans. Common people were the object of his affection, and as a result, relationships with North Korean officials turned sour. Ultimately, it was his lack of love for all people that led to him being detained.

The lesson was sobering.

Stephen started traveling in and out of North Korea to continue Pastor Kim's work, alternating one week in North Korea and one week in China, while I remained in China with our two young children and six months pregnant with our third child, Anna.

It was an extremely tense working environment as we tried to work with the same North Koreans who had witnessed Pastor Kim being detained and then expelled. In their eyes, everything we did was suspicious regardless of the reason. Also, we were only in our thirties at the time, and our North Korean counterparts did not respond well to working with such a young man in comparison to our older predecessor. The working pressure continually increased, and we felt like a typhoon had hit us.

This all started to change when Pastor Peter Kim came to visit Rason. Even though he had never met Pastor Jae-Yell Kim, he knew of him and was familiar with his work. This Pastor Kim was a pastor of a Korean American church in the Los Angeles area and had retired early to spend the rest of his life working on behalf of North Korean citizens. Although he did not live in North Korea, he visited several times a year and ministered particularly to children. He was respected by many.

After hearing rumors that Stephen was struggling to continue Pastor Jae-Yell Kim's work, Pastor Peter Kim came to China to see us in person and visit North Korea.

Without any advanced notice, he took Stephen to a meeting with senior North Korean executives and exclaimed, "From now on, I will do all my work in Rason through Mr. Yoon here, so if there is anything you would like to ask me to do, please do it through his person."

Stephen was shocked. He had little experience and not many good personal connections in North Korea. Pastor Peter Kim's sudden endorsement surprised not only us but also everyone in the room, who looked surprised because Stephen was only in his thirties. Typically, North Koreans would expect a more experienced, older man with clout to take over such a large responsibility.

But God raised us up that day through Pastor Peter Kim. Now the North Koreans looked at Stephen with esteem, knowing that this respected pastor was relying exclusively on Stephen. Through these words in that one meeting, our situation in North Korea was completely reversed. From a young man in his thirties who seemed like a nobody, Stephen became a person in North Korea whom people were instructed to serve well. It was unexpected and overwhelming, and a little bit like how Joseph must have felt as he took his place in the Pharaoh's government, or even in his role in Potiphar's house.

Pastor Peter Kim supported our ministry and was willing to act as a buffer from the sometimes stormy seas. He entrusted us with the task of building a new kindergarten, and it gave us the opportunity to establish our own good track record in North

Korea and correct some of the wrong conclusions people had made about us.

Above all, as our position changed, new opportunities for ministries opened in North Korea that had never been seen before.

We learned so much from Pastor Peter Kim, and one of the impressive things is that every time he goes into a restaurant and meets an employee, he asks for that person's name. Years later, Pastor Peter Kim can still remember that person's name and uses it when he sees them again. He also remembers that person's parents and their children's names. He can do this because once he meets a North Korean, he prays for them by name every morning.

Whenever he encounters a North Korean, they feel deeply moved by his genuine care for them, driven solely by love.

Thanks to having him as our strong umbrella, our credibility in North Korea increased, and although it has been ten years since we first met, he continues to be a vital mentor and coworker for our team and community.

Just one year after entering North Korea, we branched off from the established work we were a part of and created an independent NGO known as Sunyang Hana in Korean (IGNIS Community in English). Through this NGO, our team has expanded into more fields than ever before, and we have been able to achieve our dream of living in North Korea.

When Pastor Jae-Yell Kim was suddenly removed from us, the pillar we had relied on was gone. We felt like we were floating, like a kite that had broken its string and was tossed about in the wind of an unfamiliar land. But when we were most discouraged, God gave us a new helper in the second Pastor Kim, which allowed us to persist on our path.

At this same time, Anna arrived, and God sent us back into North Korea as a family of five, compelled by God's love, no matter what difficulties lay ahead. God had called us to share the love of Christ with the people of North Korea.

Crisis brings both danger and opportunity. When we came to North Korea, we faced many difficulties, but it also opened up an opportunity for us to sail out into a bigger sea. Through God's grace alone, we are able to hold fast at such a time and not be shaken by the wind and the rain in our lives. God was at work, and is still at work, transforming difficult situations into blessings, even in North Korea.

Perhaps you too are faced with an impossible life circumstance. Could this obstacle be turned into a blessing for you as well? This crisis you face is an opportunity for God's grace.

DON'T WALK ALONE

STEPHEN

*From him the whole body, joined and held together
by every supporting ligament, grows and builds
itself up in love, as each part does its work.*

—EPHESIANS 4:16

B y 2008, I was making regular trips to head up the humanitarian work handed over to me. It had been about a month since I had been in Rason, and although North Korea is not a democracy, it was election time, of sorts. (Voting is only a formality; there is only ever one candidate on the ballot.) Public loudspeakers in the front of our hotel broadcast propaganda about the upcoming event informing people, through songs and announcements, to vote—and whom to vote for. Like an alarm, I heard the same song at seven o'clock every morning.

At first, it was only background noise, but with the daily repetition, I soon found myself humming the tune while brushing my teeth. As I hummed along one day, I suddenly realized something: I shouldn't be working here alone.

I had come to love the people whom I worked with, but the more I served them, the more the distinction between "them" and "us" blurred. I wondered whether or not I was being indoctrinated and wondered if I would be able to maintain my faith here alone. Being in community was essential if I was not to lose myself along the way. Where there is light, darkness naturally disappears.

As you can imagine, it was not easy to find people to come to work alongside us. It was even more difficult to find people to come live with us in North Korea. I assumed people were afraid of the same things we had been afraid of before we came and worried about the things I was also wondering about now.

But still, we dreamed of a day when a small mustard seed would be planted and grow into a large tree. Our whole family was hoping and praying that someone would join us in our work. In the meantime, I focused on China. As an ally of North Korea, China shares many things politically, socially, and culturally. Through our time spent in China, I came to discover young men and women of faith who loved the Lord with great dedication. So I traveled to various house churches in China to deliver a message to young adults, challenging them to go and serve in North Korea.

One day I was having a meeting with our business investors at a coffee shop in Yanji, China, when I overheard a familiar conversation at the table next to me. The conversation between these two Chinese women indicated that they must be
Christians. After going over and introducing myself, I handed
one of the ladies my business card and asked if she could intro-
duce me to some church leaders in her Christian circle.

A few days later, I received a phone call from an unknown
man. He said that he was calling after being introduced to me by a
third party and identified himself as Pastor S. C. Kim. At the time,
he was a youth pastor in Yanji. On my next trip to China, we were
able to meet in person. I explained to him my passion for working in North Korea and that I had no one to work with. He deeply
appreciated my passion and said that his church was also praying
and preparing for work in North Korea. My excitement and joy
overflowed! It felt like I had inherited a thousand co-laborers.

Through this youth pastor, I was introduced to several young
adults, and a few of them immediately joined our team. At that
time, I did not have any grand plans or thoughts for building a
community. We just needed people to work alongside us, dream-
ing the same dream that we had for the country. Soon though, six
people (one of whom was the sister that I met at the coffee shop
that day) and our family formed a team and started working
together in North Korea building clinics, kindergartens, and
daycare centers and providing them with medical and nutri-
tional support every month. We established our own NGO with
the name Sunyang Hana.

One of the questions I often get is how we decided on the
name Sunyang Hana. At a young adult gathering in Incheon,

South Korea, I shared that I needed a name for our new organization. A couple of days later, a young man came to me explaining that he had prayed and fasted for a few days to come up with a name. Written on the slip of paper he handed to me was the word *sunyang*.

Sunyang has many meanings, but the most common meaning is "goodness," or "good light." I was so thankful for his sincere gesture that I took the name without any hesitation. Since we were longing to be partnering with others as a team, I added the word *hana*, which means "one" in Korean. So the name Sunyang Hana means "Good One." As the name suggests, our organization consists of good people gathered together as one to do good things.

We did not want our devotion to be rooted in any political or national passion, but we wanted to show through our lives very simply but clearly the Christian essence of "loving your neighbor as yourself."

The news of our new team eventually got out, and others started to join us. Some were people who were in search of their own calling, curious about life in North Korea, but others were committed individuals, dedicated to our calling. Now that more than ten years have passed, our organization has grown to about sixty field members, including both adults and children.

Sunyang Hana members come from nine different countries, including the United States, China, the Philippines, Brazil, Mongolia, Singapore, Canada, Norway, and South Korea. After becoming a global community for the purpose of sharing love with our North Korean neighbors, we adopted the name IGNIS Community in addition to our existing Korean name.

From working alone to expanding into an international NGO, branches of our nonprofit organization have been established in Seoul, Korea, and Dallas, Texas, in the United States. Donors supporting our humanitarian work come from all around the world but primarily from the United States and South Korea.

As an organization, we are not just crossing national borders but also using the avenues of various projects for legitimate ways to engage in the country beyond politics and ideology. Above all, our organization focuses on the healthy development of North Korean children in the realm of medicine, health, and education. What I am grateful for is that many people have supported humanitarian work in North Korea despite ever-changing internal and external circumstances, including the upheavals of international relations.

I once knew North Korea only as a closed country that did not allow visitors from the outside. Since the end of the Korean War, South Koreans have no longer been able to travel to and from North Korea. But the fact is that North Korea is more open than we think. Although it is uniquely a communist and socialist country, the nation's policy does not enforce national isolation. In contrast, North Korea actually actively sends their students to study overseas to develop their nation's globalization. Of course, the country is not completely open due to its highly controlled society and strict laws. But in reality, North Korea has multiple international exchanges with foreign countries. It is not a closed, imperial castle with walls designed to isolate itself.

So there is hope.

If you approach North Korea from solely a political perspective, you will be limited in what you can do. But if you approach

North Korea from a faith standpoint, united with Christians from all around the world, there are so many things that can be done. I am not just talking about a political unification on the Korean Peninsula but about what we can do now, today. Ministry in North Korea is often thought of as being dependent upon finances. But every day that I work there, I realize that money is not the key. Something else is more important. And that key is community—people who are walking together in Jesus's footsteps by faith.

I could sense from that day I was brushing my teeth that my ministry in North Korea should not be done alone; there were too many hazards to be navigated on my own. Community is necessary to affirm each other in our work, holding each other accountable spiritually and in our personal lives, so that we can work in a balanced way without becoming biased to any one side.

Most of all, in community we can be a pillar of encouragement and support for one another. When you are alone, you are fragile. If something difficult happens, it is easy to become discouraged and fall into depression or disillusionment. This unity in community is an essential element to living in North Korea. But it's also essential to living as a Christian anywhere in the world. It is through living in love and unity as a committed community that our joy is made complete and the world sees Christ in us (1 John 1:3–4, John 17:21).

One day a co-worker explained how all of a sudden feelings of isolation and negative thoughts flooded his mind, but as those feelings engulfed him, someone knocked on his door. As he opened it, he saw the familiar face of a colleague before him. He was brought out of his isolation and depression, and the negative emotions that had overtaken him disappeared in an instant.

There are many times when just being together is a strong comfort. I often wonder if I would have even been able to do what I did in North Korea if our family had been alone. The strength of our community has been so great that we have been able to stay in North Korea for over ten years.

A community does not have to be big; it just has to share a mission. Jesus himself only had twelve in his community. Even two or three people can be a community when they share their lives with one another because they are centered on Christ (Matthew 18:20). Christ does not want us to go at it alone. He wants us to be a body, the church, and to be built up and build one another up together.

SEEING
THEIR HUMANITY

STEPHEN

So God created mankind in his own image,
in the image of God he created them;
male and female he created them.

—GENESIS 1:27

Every time we meet children in North Korea—whether they are boys with dark hair and playful faces or shy girls with cheerful, bright smiles—we are grateful that we are here. As the sounds of children's laughter echo across the countryside, it reminds me of any other ordinary country. There are times when

I am tired and exhausted from work, but when I see the faces of these children, an unknown strength springs up from within me.

Where there are children, there is life.

The next generation is precious, and they are the hope for the future. It is no different in North Korea.

Among other ministries, we prioritize placing children first. Initially, the first big project our team took on was building a kindergarten for children in a small village. In North Korea, kindergarten is a two-year program for five- and six-year-olds, and the schools are built in the villages close to the homes since young children are not expected to be able to walk as far as older children can.

We went to several villages to see which area needed a kindergarten the most. There were many places in need, but I wanted to find a place that was unique, in more need than any other location. Among our options, our hearts were led to a village called Baekhak in the Sonbong district. It was a very small rural village on the outskirts of Rason.

As I was conducting my preliminary investigation, I visited an existing kindergarten in that location. It was a small building with two or three rooms made out of tiles. Since this was in June, when the rainy season began, as I opened the door and went into the classroom, I saw water everywhere. The floor was soaking wet. It was nap time, so the children were sleeping on one side of the room on top of cardboard beds to keep dry. At the time, it was a humid summer day, but I was thinking about how cold the building must be in the winter. I decided to build a new kindergarten for those children right then and there.

Because we decided that this was the place, we worked hard for almost eight months, putting all our heart into every single nail that went into the building. As the building went up for the children of the village, not only the parents but also every villager joined in the efforts.

Finally, standing two stories high, the Baekhak kindergarten was opened. When rumors spread about this beautiful new kindergarten in the middle of the countryside, parents from surrounding villages started sending their children there. Education is very important for every child in North Korea, so parents were eager to send their children to a better kindergarten farther away. The number of students suddenly increased from sixty to one-hundred-fifty.

After constructing the building, we started supporting kindergartens and daycare centers in the Rason area every month through the Lunchbox Project. Each month we provided five tons of rice to feed each child a warm lunch every day. In addition to rice, we went directly to the local markets and carefully selected side dishes and ingredients for the children's lunches.

When we visited the children, they would swarm around us, running to us and welcoming us with bright faces. Just seeing the children thrive made our hearts flutter with pure joy. Every month, as we delivered food and supplies, our relationship with the kindergarten principal and teachers deepened. Once the principal received the message that we were coming, she would roast delicious locally grown potatoes or corn and serve them to us. I still remember the savory taste to this day.

One day the principal was wiping away her tears as she showed me a letter from her son. In North Korea, military service lasts ten years, and the principal had not seen her son for several years. She was so overjoyed in receiving just a single letter from him that tears streaked her face as she read his letter to us. It was the joy and longing any mother anywhere would feel upon hearing from her child after such a long separation. I was reminded acutely that the people of North Korea are just people—the same as me and Joy, the same as you and your family.

On another visit to the kindergarten, the principal asked me if I could help her. She wanted the children to learn how to play an instrument. So the next few times I came, I brought drums and an electric keyboard. (And since electricity is scarce in North Korea, we also provided rechargeable batteries for the keyboard!)

The next time I visited, as soon as the principal saw me, she said that she had some extremely good news to share with me. One child from the kindergarten had competed in a music competition and had won first place in the Sonbong area. The next week she beamed with pride while informing us that the same student was scheduled to participate in a poetry contest.

We heard that the child won not only the city contest but also the provincial contest, and so he went on to the top stage to compete in the capital city of Pyongyang. This was huge! It was unbelievable for a child from a rural village in North Hamgyong Province to receive such an honor.

Though the village of Baekhak was an underdeveloped area and a poor environment, given an opportunity, this child's passion expanded his dreams beyond his little town to the nation's capital itself. I was thrilled as our service to this community seemed to be opening up possibilities never dreamed of before. This one motivated child taught me the importance of following through with small requests. Building the kindergarten was important, but the more significant thing was the beautiful future we were creating while working together with the villagers.

Through this simple kindergarten, the children and the entire village were changing. Hope gave birth to more hope as new talents and infinite possibilities were being discovered. With this newfound hope, we expect that this generation will grow up to instill more dreams into their own children.

I had to put down my preconceived notions about this rural, mountain village and its people and start having faith and hope in their potential.

All people are created in God's image, and He loves them all as His children. I picture God when He looks at us here on Earth like a doctor with no discrimination, with compassion for a sick patient regardless of whom his patient is. Or as a father who looks on with delight as one of his children lends a hand to her sibling.

Entering into the lives of those in this village, I was able to see that the children in the Baekhak kindergarten will grow up and eventually go to the military, that many staff at the kindergarten have children serving in the military, but that does not make these people my enemies.

As I engaged with their humanity, and my own, it dawned on me that these were not people who were thinking about war every day. They were merely people who needed a good meal, who missed their sons when they were gone, who beamed with pride for a hometown hero who won a distinguished award. They were just ordinary people living out their daily lives. Like me. Like you.

When we take away the politics and the prejudices, we begin to see the humanity inside North Korea. I believe it's the same lesson the church also needs to learn today: to look beyond the tribalism of politics, social issues, and prejudices and begin to see the people on the other side of the issues and aisles for what they are—human beings, created in God's image, living the human experience as best as they know how to—and learn to embrace and love them just as our Father in Heaven does.

NOT ACCORDING TO OUR PLANS BUT ACCORDING TO THEIR NEEDS

STEPHEN

*With respect and fear, and with sincerity of heart,
just as you would obey Christ. Obey them not only
to win their favor when their eye is on you, but as
slaves of Christ, doing the will of God from your
heart. . . as if you were serving the Lord, not people.*

—EPHESIANS 6:5–7

We established our work building kindergartens and day-care centers, but not too long after, God brought another opportunity to help to our door.

One day I was working with our North Korean counterparts on our humanitarian projects when a member from the North Korean People's Committee came to see me. The People's Committee is a branch of the North Korean government that executes and implements the policies of the policymaking arm, the Labor Party. He showed me a notebook made in North Korea of yellow-tinted paper, which had apparently been recycled multiple times before even being bound in this book. After explaining the difficulty of obtaining paper due to the lack of trees in the country, he confessed that some notebook paper even came out black due to the constant recycling of paper. As you may imagine, it is almost impossible for students to see what they write in those notebooks, especially without sufficient electricity in their classrooms.

I had never thought of serving older students before this conversation. Our focus was on providing sufficient kindergarten facilities, but instead, this officer wanted us to provide notebooks for children to study with. If we were able to provide them with paper from China, the manufacturing plant in North Korea could make their own notebooks, he added.

Since that day, with support from Pastor Peter Kim, we've supplied several tons of paper to the notebook manufacturing plant. The People's Committee made notebooks from the paper and then distributed the notebooks to kindergartens, elementary schools, and middle schools throughout the area. We provided resources valued at twenty North Korean won, so they could produce higher-quality notebooks with large sheets of clean, white paper.

Everyone was excited at the thought that the few trees in the country did not have to be cut down for the production of paper. By conserving trees, the mountains could shine again in their original glory. Countless children received the freedom to write new dreams as they received their fresh, clean notebooks.

I remember the elation and joy on people's faces the day the new notebooks came out from the factory. Previous notebooks were made with recycled paper that had been recycled so many times that the children could hardly see what they had written. With white-paper notebooks, the kids could not only see what they write but could be more creative in their drawings and descriptions. From this experience, I learned an important fact: we often try to help others in ways we think they need help. In fact, there have been times that I have felt worse after helping because those giving and those receiving help end up becoming adversaries. But by living with the people and working alongside them, I could begin to see what was really needed. This time what they needed was something that I had never thought of before.

We went into North Korea to build kindergartens, but what the villagers needed were notebooks. By serving them where they needed it most and providing notebooks, they were able to conserve and plant more trees, making their world a better place for future generations. It didn't cost us a lot of money, probably less than a kindergarten would have. But I watched our small donation transform into a valuable channel of blessing. How good it was to meet their needs on their own terms and not mine. This way we were all pleased.

Many ministries operating in North Korea have been abruptly cut short. A variety of factors contributed to projects stopping, including lack of funds, conflicts within teams, and disagreements or breaches in trust with North Korean counterparts. As a result, many are led to the misconception that North Koreans are liars, simply because reality doesn't match our plans. However, when we put their needs ahead of our own objectives, our projects often go much smoother. When we do so, there is a synergistic effect. By doing business together, not only our credibility improved but the way our donors saw North Koreans also changed for the better.

For those who want to help North Korea and are thinking about what they should do, instead of making your own plans based on what you think they need, try asking North Koreans first what their needs are.

Each person has their own love language. Some say that they feel loved when they hear compliments. Others feel loved when they receive and share gifts. And still others crave to be touched or practically served. When our love language is different from another's, even when you are expressing love, it is often not received well. Is it really loving to only love in your own way and not consider the other person's love language? Like a married couple forcing their own love language upon each other, it does not usually result in a reciprocally loving relationship. Rather than sticking with our own ways, it is appropriate to consider how we can more effectively convey God's love to North Koreans.

For Christians, salvation is only one aspect of following Christ. But that moment is only the beginning of God's work in our lives. Just as an apple seed is planted and grows into a tree that produces many apples for many years, by keeping relationships central in our work, the fruit that results will bring about many blessings that are truly unpredictable.

Sometimes those of us who serve or give can be tempted to think that these things make us superior to those whom we help, but we should know that we are just deliverymen in the kingdom of God. The deliveryman just ensures the gift is properly delivered according to the will of the sender. The recipient of the gift thanks the sender of the gift, not the deliveryman. God is the sender of blessings. We are just privileged to deliver those blessings, so we cannot think of ourselves more highly than the recipients of those blessings. Joy and I, and the people we partner with, are just delivery people, delivering God's blessings to the people in North Korea.

If only there were more workers to deliver such blessings!

11

LOVE IS JUST LOVE

STEPHEN

Love is patient, love is kind . . . It is not self-seeking.

—1 CORINTHIANS 13:4–5

On the Korean map, there is one last fishing village on the northeast border between Russia and North Korea, and that place is called Uam-ri. To get there, you have to climb a winding mountain dirt road for hours. The road is a difficult pass, so no one visits there easily, nor by chance. But since it is a coastal road that runs along the East Sea, it provides exquisite ocean scenery.

When you enter the village, the first thing that catches your eye is the squid being dried on the roofs and walls of every house. When I first came to Uam-ri, I immediately thought that it would be a good place to build a clinic. It seemed vital for village residents to receive the medical care that they needed. Otherwise, to obtain medical treatment, a person would have to drive an hour and a half, but there are no personal cars in North Korea, so it is extremely difficult for residents to get treatment. As a result, we started the long trek to bring the necessary medications and medical equipment.

The doctors at the clinic actually worked harder than I did to serve the people in their village, and I was always somewhat ashamed as I greeted them with our minimal medical support. I always left our visits determined to do more for the clinic on the next one. The doctors were always busy and delighted to treat the residents with the medicine we provided, although it was difficult because of the large number of patients to see.

Oddly enough, I enjoyed the drive from the main city of Rajin to this village. If we left early in the morning, we would arrive around lunchtime at Uam-ri. The doctor's wife at the clinic would cook a pot of flounder soup for us and wait for our arrival. After carefully preparing and serving the meal, the clinic's director would wrap dried squid caught directly from their fishing boats into a piece of paper and place it in the car for us to eat as we go.

The warm meal prepared by this countryside doctor's wife, although simple in form and variety, smelled and tasted better than a high-end restaurant. After emptying our bowls, we enjoyed watching the kids and grandkids finish their meals.

I greatly appreciated their hospitality. On each visit, I often left feeling like I received more than I gave.

What else could be done there? I thought on my drive home.

Although we had built a clinic, medicine was severely lacking. The medicine we supplied was brought in from China and the United States, but bringing medicine across the border was always a stressful event. About twenty to thirty percent of the medicine was confiscated at the border.

But if we had the will, there always seemed to be a way.

While I was thinking about the need for medicine, I realized that another American had set up a pharmaceutical company in the Rason area. His company brought in raw ingredients to be manufactured into medicine in North Korea. Thankfully, through this pharmaceutical company, we were able to provide medicines like antibiotics, aspirin, and painkillers for only the cost of ingredients.

Typically, pharmaceutical costs are high and often unaffordable because they include the cost of advertisement, research, and development, as well as packaging. But thanks to this pharmaceutical enterprise, medicine was able to be supplied much more easily and cheaply to the countryside clinics. In this way, it was possible to provide a variety of medicines at a significantly reduced cost. With $300, I could deliver four large boxes of medicine to a clinic.

Time and time again, I bore witness to God's love that flowed out for the people of North Korea: the kind of attending, fatherly love that takes pleasure in watching your children eat, seeing the joy in their faces as they became satisfactorily full. God's love comes from a father's heart, which is always thinking about what is needed, what can be done. As I looked through God's eyes, I too had the same desires and heart for these people. I did not originally have these desires. It was only Christ in me teaching me these things.

"Which of you, if his son asks for bread, will give him a stone?" (Matthew 7:9). If this is the heart of a worldly father, how much more does our Heavenly Father give good gifts to his children, even to his children in North Korea? Every day North Koreans are learning how to recognize and receive God's love.

The more your love grows, the more capacity your love has. Love is as big as you express, receive, or share it. Where I gave love, I also received love in return. The more I experienced how to love, the more I laid down my old preconceived notions of love. As I grew up, love was rooted in a self-focused notion that produced a feeling of warmth and gratification. But this was different. This kind of love demonstrated itself through selfless hospitality. The more I received love, the more I felt compelled to pay it back by living with the people.

We usually expect to be rewarded for our efforts. The more I give, the more I tend to hope that the other side will reciprocate in kind. But because of these expectations, there are times when we feel a sense of frustration that the exchange does not seem fair, and we begin to lose our purpose. At first, it feels like we are freely giving love, but after a while, that feeling can turn into resentment.

In truth, we don't need to worry about how much love we give or get. It is God who repays us and rewards us for our giving. While working in North Korea, as I let go of my expectations, love became just love. Not for self-reward or gratification or any reason at all. Love is simply just love.

THE PARADOX OF EMPTY POCKETS

STEPHEN

*My grace is sufficient for you, for my
power is made perfect in weakness.*

—2 CORINTHIANS 12:9

It was the summer of 2008 when the Chinese government restricted all rice from being exported abroad because of fluctuating prices of rice. They hoped that blocking exports would help temporarily stabilize the market. This might not have affected you or your family, but it sent shock waves through North Korea.

Up until then, the price of rice in North Korea was about 800 North Korean won per kilogram, but because of the blocked imports, the price suddenly rose to 3,000 won, three or four times higher. Many people in North Korea remember vividly the famine they experienced in the 1990s when droughts and floods caused famine in the land, starving many to death.

The sudden astronomical rice prices shocked many, especially in rural areas where resources are limited.

I too was nervous about the food situation in North Korea.

Normally, rice was provided to kindergartens by the government, but due to inflation, rice was scarce and not sent to kindergartens. In order to solve the food shortage, kindergartens told the parents that each child would be responsible for bringing a bag of rice from home to feed the children lunch. But not many houses were capable of doing this. Still, these children needed an education along with at least one good, hot meal. Our North Korean guide asked Sunyang Hana to provide it.

At that time, one ton of rice cost approximately $600. It would take at least five tons of rice to provide food for these children. We did not have that kind of money. Our ministry was just beginning, so our team did not have much funds. After hearing our guide's explanation, I replied that I would pray for the money. If money came in, then we could feed the children.

So our team began to pray. We prayed that the Lord would provide us with the money we needed to buy rice for the children. In the meantime, there was a foreign congregation at the Beijing International Church (BICF) in China. I visited a staff member of the church, and after briefly sharing our ministry update, the church offered to donate $9,000 to feed the kindergarten children. We were both delighted and surprised. This was the exact amount we needed to start the program.

Once the money came in, we bought five tons of rice for the Rajin area to start a lunchbox program that provided lunches to kindergarten children. We needed $3,000 a month to feed all the children, and after three months, that generous donation was completely spent.

On the way back from buying our last installment of rice, I sadly told our North Korean guide that I didn't have any money left for the next month. Knowing that there was nothing he could do about it, our guide went back with a sad and heavy heart. You could see on his face the burden that weighed upon him now that the children might not have sufficient rations.

But something strange happened.

When I got home that day, I discovered that there was approximately $5,000 in my Korean bank account—and I had no idea where it came from.

Excited to have more funds, and without waiting to see if it was some mistake, I immediately bought more rice and side dishes to distribute to the kindergartens. Then the next month, another $5,000 came in. I wondered who was sending the funds, so I asked those around me, but everyone said that they knew nothing about the donation.

Many months later, when I met a minister from a church in Seoul, I told the pastor about the mysterious donations coming in. With a smile, he informed me that he had given my bank account information to a young man in his church. This young man worked in the stock market, and he wanted to help North Korean children. The company he worked for was a Christian company, and one day, at the company's prayer meeting, the president of the company heard from him how we had been helping children in North Korea. God stirred the president's heart to use a portion of the company profits from the year before to support children in North Korea. Rather than providing funds through our acquaintances, this man, whom we had never met, sent us the funds to feed children, just from hearing one brief prayer request. He continued to send $5,000 a month for an entire year. We were able to provide lunches for the children as well as necessary school supplies, from the generosity of a person we'd never even met.

What is even more surprising is that for the next seven years, without fail, every month our team was supplied with the funds needed to feed these children, and the lunchbox program continued.

Our organization was not an expert in fundraising. Our team was made up of mostly young adults in their twenties and thirties. Many of them were Chinese nationals who had neither access to funds nor experience with fundraising. We had a lot more passion than connections!

Whenever there was a need like this, I would sit down and, to be honest, despair about the lack of funds. Then I'd rely on my problem-solving and persuasion skills, make a list of people who could potentially contribute to the cause, and reach out to them with requests.

But seldom did these people financially support us.

Rather, finances typically came through people I met by chance or who heard about us from church or friends and whom we didn't even know—people God had prepared to do this good work with us by financially supporting our efforts.

I began to use funding as a way of discerning if we should take on a project. If the Lord gave me the money for the project, that was His sign of approval for us to do it. As a result, I learned to live in connection with Him and by relying upon the Lord's provision, moment by moment. Doing so calmed my fears and my anxious striving.

Just like George Mueller, I learned that God answers prayers at just the right time so that no one will go hungry. Not one of our team's ministries collapsed due to a lack of funds.

God's fatherly love raised up Christians to provide for us and the people we came to serve.

As of 2024, sixteen kindergarten and daycare facilities and six rural clinics have been built. Between 1,000 to 3,000 children are provided lunch every day. In addition, about 200 teachers and doctors have received rice and soybean oil every month for their families' use.

Like many ministries, usually at the end of every year, our project accounts have a zero-dollar balance. Without any funds in the bank, we plan our projects and estimate our budget for the next year by faith. This lack of funds trains us to confess our weaknesses and depend upon the Lord. Amazingly, our funds are refilled each year, and by the end of it, we have often been able to complete what we've planned and budgeted to do.

The individuals and groups who have supported our work for the past seventeen years have been our partners in our ministry. Our whole community has been trained to be bold in the midst of lacking finances and to be filled with God's amazing grace and provision.

North Koreans can survive without us. God called us to this land to show us and strengthen our own weaknesses and learn to depend more upon Him.

In this too, I have received more than I have given. This is the paradox of blessing that I enjoy by living and working in North Korea.

BUILDING A
FOUNDATION OF LOVE

STEPHEN

So do not fear, for I am with you; do not be dismayed,
for I am your God. I will strengthen you and help
you; I will uphold you with my righteous right hand.

—ISAIAH 41:10

In the middle of our second year in North Korea, I was wearing two layers of clothes on top of my long underwear. I also had on a winter coat, a scarf, and a blanket, but all those layers were still not enough to keep me warm. As I woke up in my hotel bed, my whole body ached from the cold. Even the toilet had frozen over. It was early spring according to the calendar, but the temperature was still below freezing. Most of the hotel's heating relied upon electricity, but since electricity is unreliable, some mornings we could still see our breath in the air indoors as we talked.

What in the world am I doing here right now? I pondered. *I should just go back to our house in China where my wife and children are waiting. Why am I living here alone, having such a hard time?*

Until our whole family could obtain resident visas, I traveled back and forth from where they were in our residence across the border in China to the current project our organization was working on in North Korea.

This day I was at a construction site fighting over logistics with our North Korean counterparts. I had a steep learning curve to overcome as my expertise was not in construction, and I felt obligated to make sure funds were appropriately allocated.

My body felt more exhausted than usual, and I wondered, *Am I here to fight? How am I going to convey God's love by arguing like this? Why is working with the North Korean officials so difficult? How am I being a witness to the Lord as I act like this?* I also wondered, *Why is this job so difficult?*

I had come to North Korea with great enthusiasm, but maintaining it was not as easy as I had anticipated.

As I worked alongside unfamiliar people on projects outside my expertise, my body and mind became drained. I was a doctor who most often worked as a foreman. The more my worries about funding and construction details and my ability to manage it all piled up, the more discouraged I became.

Life in North Korea was like living on a roller coaster, with constant ups and downs and unexpected twists and turns. One project might have sufficient funds, but then another obstacle would arise. The constant problem-shooting, demand for fund-raising, overcoming miscommunication and misunderstand-ings with North Korean counterparts, and the intense spiritual atmosphere could drain a person.

To cool my head for a while, I walked around the construction site and began to pray quietly. All of a sudden, something caught my eye. It was a cross. I was so confused.

What in the blazes is a cross doing here?

I moved in to take a closer look. There, in plain sight, was a wooden cross standing on the roof of a building. Unbelievable! I was so startled I stopped and stood there. In that moment, it was as if God was speaking to me.

I am here, so don't be discouraged.

I burst into tears.

In that moment, I needed some encouragement, and God came to me. He comforted me as He confirmed to me that He was with me in North Korea—amid the need, confusion, frustration, and overwhelm I was feeling.

As I cried, a beautiful thought bubbled up in my mind.

You may think that you are just building a kindergarten or a few clinics in this land, but these are not just buildings. With every brick you lay, you are building a foundation for the love of God.

I don't know if that was my realization or a comforting mes-sage from the Lord, but from that moment on, I knew that the work that I did was work that God had entrusted to me. Although the journey was difficult, I realized once again that I was there for God to bless that land.

As I walked to the front of the building to take an even closer look at what I saw, I realized that what I was looking at was actually a pole with an electric cord wrapped around it! But that just goes to show that God can use *anything* to communicate His message to someone who needs to hear it.

After this encounter, a new energy sprang up from within me. God reminded me that this was not a physical battle but that just my presence there had spiritual significance. God was opening up my eyes to not focus on the problems or the obstacles but to focus on Him and on the people God had placed in my path. He maximized my resilience.

The way that I looked at our North Korean counterparts also changed. I began to see them as valuable partners instead of obstacles to argue with, and I endeavored to build meaningful relationships with them. Of course, there were still frustrations and difficulties that arose from our work, thorns and thistles planted at the fall. But these challenges came and went in waves. Whenever frustrations arose, I would simply pray more. I would pray for God to pour out upon this earth all of who He is.

When the Israelites were taken into captivity in Babylon, God instructed them to "seek the peace and prosperity of the city to which I have carried you into exile. Pray to the Lord for it, because if it prospers, you too will prosper" (Jeremiah 29:7).

God's intention is to bless, not to curse.

Even those who hurt us or persecute us should be blessed (Matthew 5:44). This is God's will because it leads us to a peaceful and godly life (1 Timothy 2:2).

God's heart is to bless North Koreans, not to curse them. Our hearts should align with His.

14

BY THIS, THEY'LL KNOW YOU'RE MY DISCIPLES

STEPHEN

A new command I give you: Love one another. As I have loved you, so you must love one another. By this everyone will know that you are my disciples, if you love one another.

—JOHN 13:34–35

Just a few years prior, I was treating chiropractic patients in the United States, and now, in Rajin, I was overseeing construction projects in North Korea. It had been like learning a new language as an adult: fumbling, awkward, and stilted.

Since none of us on our team had construction expertise, this task was very difficult for us.

In addition to that, we were advised by our predecessors, "You need to be careful about working in North Korea. They have a habit of stealing, so you will need to make sure that your materials do not get stolen. Since these buildings are being built with church donations, if someone steals those materials, you are wasting God's money."

That felt like a heavy charge. After hearing these words, these building projects became that much greater of a burden for me to handle.

Our team met daily for both prayer and project management. The topic of our conversation was often how we could properly protect our resources in order not to be robbed or taken advantage of by the North Koreans. Due to some advice we received, we "played hardball" with our North Korean counterparts on everything, even though we were not construction experts. We were tough and hard-edged about all the details we could be: permits, costs, personnel, schedules, and anything and everything we could so as not to be taken advantage of or worse.

Daily, we strategized about how we should navigate the day as the construction proceeded, attacking the quality of their work and defending the use of our funds. The projects would proceed accordingly, and we believed that we might just know what we were doing. But soon the North Korean officials who worked with us would avoid us. They would push off our projects until later, and they became increasingly reluctant to talk with us. Because of our argumentative posture, fighting at the end of every word, they said, they no longer wanted to deal with us.

We thought we were being shrewd as serpents, not letting anyone cheat or take advantage of us, but it was affecting our team dynamics as well. As we fought with North Koreans to see our projects succeed, we discovered that the relationships within our team turned aggressive and militant. Those who showed up a little late to meetings were scolded, and we became judgmental toward those in our team who made honest mistakes. We used piercing thorns in the words we spoke to each other and gave each other disapproving looks.

After a while, the way we treated each other within our team resembled the way we treated North Koreans. When we finally realized this, we felt a serious sense of crisis, like a train running off its track. Our community started with a heart to love and serve North Koreans, but if even we, who were brothers and sisters in Christ, could not forgive and love one another, then how could we say that we loved the North Koreans?

During a morning prayer and project meeting, God reminded us through the prayer of His vision for a community in John 13.

"A new command I give you. Love one another. As I have loved you, so you must love one another. By this all men will know that you are my disciples, if you love one another" (John 13:34–35).

These words struck our hearts like lightning. We knelt down and repented. We realized that we had to examine ourselves first before we judged the right or wrong of the North Koreans.

We had to redefine what our priorities were. Protection and productivity no longer were our priorities. Instead, our priorities became people and relationships. Our goal was to create a warm, welcoming environment for kindergarten children who had to study in poor conditions during the frigid winter. But we had been working vigilantly and with suspicion toward anyone and anything we encountered on the way, including each other and our North Korean counterparts. In turn, the North Koreans who worked with us treated us the same way. Suspicions grew even deeper and further penetrated our community.

God was teaching us through that prayer that He did not just send us to North Korea to build buildings but that He was first and foremost calling us to be disciples who resembled Him. It was our duty to let the world know the love of God by loving one another. The moment we accepted the essence of the gospel, we experienced God's grace restored to our team and community.

Since that day, our community's motto has become, "Let us do well first." It means we should do well in our own team first before we criticize others. It was our reminder to take the plank out of our own eyes before we attempted to remove the speck from another's.

How hypocritical it was to think that we could teach North Koreans how to love and care for one another when we couldn't do it ourselves. Before saying that we loved North Korean children, we decided that we should first love one another. We needed to be more like Jesus, not be more effective in our work.

Soon after this revelation and conviction, Father Ben Torrey from Jesus Abbey in Taebaek, South Korea, introduced me to the community living there. Jesus Abbey is an Anglican community founded in 1965 by an American missionary. It is a Christian laboratory of sorts that focuses on a personal relationship with God, relationships among believers within the Christian community, and experimenting with relationships between the Christian community and non-Christian society.

I got my first glimpse of a monastic community in action. I was challenged by seeing people who had given up everything in the world for the sake of living together as one body in Christ.

"How could such a life be possible?" I wondered.

But then, by "coincidence," I saw that a visiting professor from a university was providing marital counseling and conflict resolution guidance for the Jesus Abbey.

"Why would such a beautiful community need help from an outside counselor?"

The professor smiled and said that the people who lived there were unable to resolve conflicts on their own, more thorns and thistles that were planted by the fall. Even behind these cloistered walls, there was conflict, envy, and strife. And these men and women needed help to work through their issues with each other.

It turned out that the community did not mean that everyone lived harmoniously, united on all issues, all the time. Even the best community experiences conflicts and difficulties.

Like in our team, many groups working in North Korea prioritized the success of their projects, and sometimes the by-products of this success were relational conflicts and wounds. These groups and individuals came to North Korea claiming that they were members of the body of Christ, but sometimes they wouldn't even face one another due to interpersonal conflict. Meanwhile, North Koreans just laughed at the spectacle the Christians put on.

North Koreans, like South Koreans, are passionate and tend to argue a lot, but due to their circumstances, they also know that they still have to live together, so they usually drink and move on. Unfortunately, though, once Christians make enemies, they stay enemies until the very end, even when that enemy is another Christian.

I took what I had seen back to the team, and we meditated our hearts and minds around God's command that we "love one another." We decided that our community should function as a family. As we did, our relationships with each other and our North Korean counterparts, which had been cold, were gradually restored.

One of our North Korean supervisors was transferred to another department, and the day before he left his position with us, he came to me. It was a sad parting since, by this time, we had worked and lived together for over three years. While we were strolling on the beach together, saying our goodbyes, he carefully confided his feelings to me.

"Mr. Yoon, when I first was assigned as your counterpart, I thought that you were very bad people. However, after observing you closely, I learned a new fact. That is that you are not all bad people. Although I am being transferred and cannot work with you anymore, I will do my best to help you from whatever position I have."

It was an unexpected promise. At one time we had hated one another and looked at each other with darting glares. But now our eyes met, wet with tears, as we said goodbye with a warm final handshake.

We are still learning how to "love one another." Most often we hurt and are hurt most by the people closest to us, such as our parents, our brothers, our sisters, or even those we go to church with, more so than people who are distant from us like North Koreans. But it is hypocritical to skip loving your neighbor and try loving the stranger, like North Koreans, instead.

We first went to North Korea to help meet their needs, but as we did, we were discovering that North Korea was not changing because of what we brought to it. We might have needed more fixing than what North Koreans needed us to fix.

We learned that as God first loved us, by first loving each other, those on the outside would see the love of Jesus in us.

When you are with a militant person, you become militant. When you are with a judgmental person, you judge more. But when you are with a loving person, you become love. What message are you sending to those you live, work, and worship with? Is there someone in your life you don't think you could possibly love? What if you just began praying for that person every day? What might happen, not only for them but for you too?

IT NEVER GOES
AS PLANNED

STEPHEN

"For my thoughts are not your thoughts, neither
are your ways my ways," declares the LORD.

—ISAIAH 55:8

One of the most frequent questions we get asked is, "Why did you ever start a shoe manufacturing company?"

It's a fair question. I am a medical professional, and Joy was a science teacher.

A shoe manufacturing company was not what we had in mind for our work in North Korea. When my father abruptly—and shockingly—decided to join us in our move, he brought with him twenty-five years of experience in running a shoe factory in South Korea. At the time, I had no idea how many areas a shoe factory could impact, but it is further proof that work does not need to be "Christian" work to impact a community and people with His love.

When I visited Rason for the first time, I told the North Korean officials that my father was joining us and explained his work experience to them. They gladly invited him to help them manufacture shoes in their "factory." He accepted their offer, and by doing so, it allowed us to obtain resident visas and live in North Korea as a family.

We did not have the large amount of funds required to start our own factory, so we initially partnered with the existing Rason Shoe Factory, with the intention to manufacture shoes for export. In this joint venture, North Korea would provide labor, and we would provide raw materials and manufacturing facilities. We paid the workers per shoe that passed the quality inspection.

However, when I visited the existing North Korean factory, I saw there was no equipment for making shoes. Instead of conveyor belts and machinery, I just saw female employees sitting on the ground, laying shredded dried pollack on plastic sheets covering the ground. I wondered if this was ever a shoe factory at all.

Because of the lack of raw materials or operating machinery available to use in the factory, many of those who worked there lost their jobs. The company manager said that they were now making money by selling dried pollack because there was no other work for them and they had to do something.

I called a meeting with the shoe company manager and expressed that we hoped to run the factory again to produce shoes. As I did, color started coming back into people's faces, and smiles turned up the corners of their mouths. We were excited too, but once again, we had to start from scratch.

Over the next several months, we worked tirelessly to make the factory operational again. A large portion of that work was done by my father, who spearheaded creating business proposals, finding investors, and doing technical research for raw materials. Soon we had created a solid business plan and started looking for investors. We decided to lean into my father's experience making winter snow boots, as North Koreans typically only wore dress shoes or simple canvas shoes and had nothing for the cold winter months. One pair could be made by attaching the material upper boot to a rubber toe and outsole. Soon the shoe factory was creating more jobs than ever expected. It was a great opportunity for North Korean women who knew how to operate a sewing machine to manufacture shoes. In fact, many women felt privileged and proud to be able to directly contribute to their family's finances with their work.

In the early days, we exported shoes to China, Mongolia, and Switzerland. UNICEF ordered a large number of shoes from us for earthquake victims in Sichuan, China. World Vision and Good Neighbors also ordered shoes for children in Mongolia and Africa through us. The North Korean workers took great pride in these exports, which were marked "Made in the DPRK," and were able to help people around the globe.

While our shoe factory was busy, a few local women came and asked to get twenty pairs of shoes at cost as they wanted to start their own businesses selling shoes but did not have the money for the initial inventory. These women promised that they would pay back the money after they sold the shoes. Naturally, we were skeptical if we'd ever see the women again, let alone any money, but I admired their entrepreneurial spirit and ingenuity. Since we were already busy with preexisting orders, we told the women we simply couldn't meet the additional demand. As it was, the factory was operating around the clock to meet the deadline for the volume of shoes needed for export.

In late 2010, in the midst of our successful operations, a crisis arose. Conflict and tensions between the two Koreas climaxed, and the UN and US sanctions against North Korea tightened. With the intention of preventing North Korea's overseas revenue, strict regulations were put into place to prevent further economic development. All products labeled "Made in the DPRK" were banned from being sold overseas. As a result, our exports were cut off overnight, and the shoe factory took a huge blow. We pivoted to selling our shoes in North Korea, but the products piled up in the warehouse, the workers lost their jobs, and the factory shut down. Economic sanctions that were levied to impact the North Korean government were instead harming these local women and impacting their ability to provide for their families.

We were at a loss as to how to resolve the situation.

Around that same time, as we visited the kindergartens that we supported, I noticed the children's shoes. After thinking about shoes for eight hours a day for three years while running the factory, I suppose it was only natural for me to notice the children's footwear.

Despite it being winter, some children wore plastic or canvas shoes with no insulation or water resistance that offered little guard from frostbite. As I looked at their feet, I remembered that the factory's winter shoes were currently piled up in the warehouse.

Perhaps we could solve both problems at once.

I contacted the pastor from our supporting church, and I explained the situation to him. A few days later, his church sent me $10,000 to buy shoes for these local children. The children were able to wear warm winter shoes, and we were able to restart our factory. The women returned to work, and the shoe donation project was birthed, becoming one of the most important projects our team would run.

While we had intended to export the shoes, we ended up sharing them with local children instead. God brought something wonderful out of our thwarted plans. Through this unexpected opportunity, children's snow boots have been distributed throughout the entire nation of North Korea thanks to the support of many donors. When I see the smiles of the children who receive our snow boots, the warmth of my own heart naturally rises.

In addition, another unplanned path to bless others opened up for us. The women who had come to us months earlier looking for twenty pairs of shoes came back. This time, with a surplus of shoes in our warehouse, we gave them what they needed.

A few weeks later, something amazing happened. The women came back to the factory and paid us back the cost of the shoes. We were not only surprised; we were moved. I thought our losses would be unavoidable. It turned out that these women not only sold the shoes, but these initial shoes turned enough profit for them so they could each start their own shoe-selling businesses. Over the next year, they took this initial investment of what amounted to about $3 and turned it into $80,000 in revenue in one year. These ladies also ended up being the avenue for our shoe company to venture into the North Korean domestic market!

Our unanticipated foray into a type of microfinancing changed these women's lives and helped us build trust with the local community. We never planned any of this. It was purely God's work turning struggle into blessings.

His ways are not our ways, but they are always better.

The shoe factory will never be in the Fortune 500 or sell its stock on Wall Street, but it is a miraculous company, one we've built side by side with North Koreans for North Koreans. It makes very little money, but the work has been worth it because of the people locally and around the world we have been able to help through it.

It's funny to think that all this resulted from my father's unanswered prayer to stop us from going to North Korea. God truly does more than we can ask or imagine (Ephesians 3:30).

RELATIONAL
BREAKTHROUGHS

J O Y

I consider that our present sufferings are not worth comparing with the glory that will be revealed in us.

—ROMANS 8:18

Doing business anywhere is not easy, but it was especially difficult doing business as a foreigner in North Korea. Because we first started the shoe company as a joint venture, we needed a company in China to sign the contract with the Rason shoe factory. As a result, we set up our main office in Yanji, China, and called it the Yanji Sunyang Shoe Industry Co., Ltd. Then we opened a branch in Rason and named it Sunyang Hana Trading Company.

When doing business in North Korea, there were times when some departments made unreasonable demands. There were also times when things became extra difficult, and we received more criticism from government officials and agencies because we were foreign Christians operating in North Korea. At times like these, our company manager would come to our defense and advocate for us against these unfounded accusations from North Korean officials.

Our company manager was a North Korean woman who came to work for us when she was in her twenties. She was an energetic woman with petite features and a tenacious spirit. She has now been in charge of operations for over ten years. Since she was a native and we were foreigners, among her roles had been protecting us from unfounded accusations and helping us effectively negotiate the unofficial demands and requests asked of us, which were often above and beyond the legal requirements. Since North Korea is a country that operates less "by the book" and more on a relational currency, negotiating the politics of these requests was something we didn't anticipate needing her help in but have benefited greatly from having.

If the company made an error, or an employee offended the government, we could be publicly criticized and kicked out of the country. In the communist system, public criticism is an integral part of the social structure. Every Saturday morning, people are required to attend small group meetings based on their workplace, school, or neighborhood. During these meetings, individuals receive training on current events and political agendas and participate in public criticisms designed to hold each other accountable for achieving personal and national goals.

For a foreign company operating in this context, errors or offenses could lead to public shaming, potentially resulting in the revocation of our business license or the cancellation of visas. There was a fine line we were always walking to maintain our ability to operate in the country, but even in the midst of hardship, our manager would encourage us and spur us on.

Always tight-lipped and polite, she never showed us how challenging her role was. We were often unaware of the issues she was faced with to keep the company running. Later we would hear from our business counterparts or people in governmental agencies of the issues our manager had faced, and we would learn how hard she had worked for our company. She said she never had any regrets, though, as she struggled through solving all our company's problems.

She consistently went above and beyond to argue our case and negotiate on our behalf.

There was once a time when the factory was busy but still did not make enough money to pay all the wages. Even if a lot of shoes were sold in the market, oftentimes our company would lose between 50 to 100 million Korean won a year. If our company could not pay our employees' monthly wages, our company could be evicted from Rason City and branded as a bad company.

Knowing the company's situation better than anyone else, our manager borrowed money from people she knew to keep it from collapsing. Thanks to her ingenuity, the company overcame many hardships. This dedication, commitment, and concern made her more than an employee; she also became our close friend.

Looking back, we can see that the reason we were able to build trust with North Koreans was because they were equally committed to us as we were to them.

The most difficult part of running the shoe factory was having to move. In the ten years our shoe company operated, we had to move the company three times. The factory building was provided by North Korea, so the land and the building on which we operated were not ours. So if they told us to move locations, we had to move. Usually, we would receive just a week's notice that our company had to relocate to another factory building. One time our entire company had to move within just three days. If we did not comply, we would have to shut down.

It is said that moving is one of the top stressors that people experience. It's truly exhausting to pack everything, move it, and unpack it in its new location. This is true for any household, but it was even more stressful moving our company. The cost of moving was so high that we lost money every time we were required to move, but we were powerless to do anything about it.

In this stressful, chaotic transition, it was easy for us to be frazzled. But our team prayed together, trying not to fall apart, and maintained our first love for this land and her people. Despite having to move, we kept our promises to the North Korean people, and we worked hard to prevent our local employees from losing their jobs.

Our manager watched closely how we responded to all these circumstances.

One day she came to me and said, "It's amazing that you have overcome so many difficulties. Thank you for being here with us. Without you, many of our employees would have been in a very difficult situation, but I want you to know how grateful our employees are for you."

She was always polite and professional with us, but these were the first words of acknowledgment and thanks she had given. I was so grateful. Her words of appreciation and acknowledgment encouraged me.

"Thank you for being with us and for overcoming this together," I responded.

A simple breakthrough with just one person is a great harvest in North Korea. Although we put a lot of time and energy into our projects, our ultimate desire was for God to touch the lives of people.

Because we incarnated into their world and shared in their difficulties, helping where we could, the employees and community we worked in opened their hearts and accepted us, even though we were outsiders.

The first thing my father-in-law did when he signed the contract with the shoe factory was to set up a cafeteria for the employees. It was the best thing he could have done. When we first visited the existing shoe factory and saw the women shredding fish, we knew there were more important things that needed to be done before we got to work. As soon as our company manager was hired, she saw my father-in-law's act and knew what kind of man he was.

Although he had experienced the Korean War, my father-in-law put people first before the project. His hard heart of not wanting anything to do with North Korea was changed, and he actually became the person on our team who spent the most time in North Korea. He treated the shoe company workers like his own family members and spent large amounts of time with our local counterparts. People, we all learned, despite all their failures and frustrations, are the most precious fruit of all.

UNITY THROUGH DIFFICULTY

J O Y

*If one part suffers, every part suffers with it; if
one part is honored, every part rejoices with it.*

—1 CORINTHIANS 12:26

There are many peaks and valleys in each of our lives, but in the midst of crises or dark times, the bottom is not truly the bottom for believers.

In December of our third year working in North Korea, I drove from our base in China to the Yanji National Medical Center for a routine medical exam that I was required to get to renew my Chinese visa. During the exam, the technicians discovered a lump around my kidney and liver. At first we ignored the thought that it might be something serious. But when we went to pick up my test results, the technician was waiting for us. She wanted to talk with me and get me to promise that I would follow up with a more thorough exam at the hospital. Because of her urgency, we immediately made an appointment at the hospital.

The next day we discovered that I had a 2.5 cm tumor in my kidney and a fluid-filled sac next to my liver. After more tests, we discovered that the tumor was rapidly growing and that I had stage-three cancer. Renal cancer usually does not display any symptoms until the cancer has metastasized to other tissues. We were in complete shock. The two of us left our children in the care of our teammates in China and traveled to South Korea for immediate surgery.

Two weeks after surgery, which was on Christmas Eve, Stephen's father traveled with all three of our children to reunite the family in South Korea as I recovered. We had missed family Christmas but did our best to make up for the holiday by celebrating in guest housing provided generously by a local church. It took a full month for me to recover before having my drainage tube and staples removed.

Before this medical emergency, we had been anticipating our first trip home to the United States in three years. Once I was well enough to travel, we boarded the plane for Chicago to see our family. A month later, as we were traveling, speaking at churches, we got a call from one of our teammates in China.

Our team member, Mr. Jung, who was supervising our humanitarian work in North Korea while we were in the United

States, had suddenly passed away from a heart attack. The team did the best they could to comfort his shocked and grieving wife and manage funeral details. Most of our teammates were still in their twenties, so it was a stressful time for everyone as no one had dealt with this kind of situation before. It was also an extremely sensitive situation because Mr. Jung, an American citizen, passed away immediately after returning to China from a trip to North Korea.

It was heartbreaking that we could not immediately travel to China to be with the rest of our team and grieve with them. Our Chinese visas expired while we were in the United States, and it would take several days, at the minimum, and several trips to the Chinese embassy to renew them. As leaders, we felt the urgency of being with our team during this tragic time. For three months, we waited to return to China.

When we arrived, we grieved Mr. Jung's death together, and within one month of our return, our team was impacted by four major traffic accidents. But although the cars were completely totaled, the cars' occupants amazingly escaped with only minor injuries. These almost unbearable, tragic events, one after another, left scars within our community and upon the hearts and minds of our young team members.

We suffered from psychological distress. It was as if Satan was mocking us, tempting us to believe he was stronger than God's protection. But nothing could separate us from God's love.

When our minds and emotions were spent and used, we found a way to rise again: prayer. We fasted and prayed for a spiritual breakthrough and physical protection for our team. Together we confessed that we were weak but that God was stronger than it all. We acknowledged that spiritual forces were trying to bring us down but that God had already won the victory. We trusted God's work was not finished yet. We believed that God still had a plan for us and that greater things were yet to come. Through these challenging events and the gathering in prayer, our team was preserved, strengthened, and united in our calling.

In 2012, Pastor Joseph, a Korean American minister, was detained in North Korea. Pastor Joseph was a representative of a major ministry group and gave lectures on engaging in overseas ministry throughout Korea. After one of his lectures on North Korean engagement, a man came up to him and gave him a letter explaining that he also was engaged in reaching out to North Koreans. As he spoke, Pastor Joseph became aware that this man's work with Korean defectors posed great risk to Pastor Joseph. Pastor Joseph politely declined to engage in the conversation further, explaining that, from what the man had shared, their two ministries were not aligned. But Pastor Joseph slipped the letter into his notebook and forgot about it. As he crossed the border into Rason, North Korea, with some members of our team, this very sensitive letter was discovered and implicated Pastor Joseph and our entire team in illegal engagement with defectors.

Upon hearing the news about this incident, Stephen rushed into Rason. When he saw our teammates, he was quite surprised. All of our team members were in the investigator's room with Pastor Joseph. They were begging the authorities to release him and arrest them instead. Pastor Joseph emphatically insisted that he had nothing to do with the contents of the letter. Our team did not relent until Pastor Joseph was proven innocent. This seriously dangerous situation could have led to his being charged with espionage. Yet not one of our teammates fled. They all stood by Pastor Joseph.

Just as each member of the body is one, when one member suffers, all the members suffer together. When one member is glorified, then all the members rejoice together (1 Corinthians 12:18–27).

Because of having experienced the love of Christ, our team members were also willing to give up their rights and even their lives for their brother in Christ.

Fortunately, Pastor Joseph was released safely, and it was through these crises that we truly felt our community becoming one. It was a miracle that all of our teammates stood together without fail. If we had not stood together at that moment, we wouldn't still be here today.

To share the gospel here is not a Bible study or the distribution of tracts. It demonstrates the love and sacrifice of Christ Jesus and the beauty of the community of faith, just by the way we live.

Maybe North Korea isn't that different from America today after all?

GOD IS ALIVE IN NORTH KOREA

STEPHEN

*These signs will accompany those who
believe . . . They will place their hands on
sick people, and they will get well.*

—MARK 16:17–18

On my second visit to North Korea in the summer of 2007, I
planned on staying for a month. I had heard that foreign
doctors are usually not allowed to treat North Koreans. So I had no
expectation to treat local patients. However, as soon as I entered
North Korea, I was unexpectedly asked by my North Korean guide
to treat patients the next day on Sunday.

Since we practiced the Sabbath, Pastor Jae-Yell Kim request-ed our guide to let us rest the following day in order to worship and then start treatment on Monday. I was shocked at his bold-ness. It seemed risky to tell the North Koreans that; however, our guide obediently agreed.

During our Sunday fellowship time together, God gave me a special message: "These signs will accompany those who believe . . . They will place their hands on sick people, and they will get well" (Mark 16:17–18).

The last part of the verse captured my heart. I felt that God was going to do an incredible miracle, so I started praying for the patients that I would see the next day. I prayed for them to be healed. However, I also selfishly prayed that only young, easy-to-treat patients would come and that all chronically ill patients would stay home because I knew that my chiropractic treatment would have the best results in these cases. I prayed sincerely and urgently, but self-centered, as I believed the answer to my prayer depended on my skills and strength.

When I got to the hospital early in the morning, people were already lining up outside the hospital door. But contrary to my prayer the night before, most of them were elderly and appeared chronically ill. These patients would require several months of intensive treatment or surgery, which I knew was not an option.

I began to resent God for not answering my prayers. My guide led me to an upstairs treatment room. People welcomed me as I came in. There were high expectations for me as a for-eign doctor, which felt like enormous pressure to me. Ten North Korean doctors were assigned to me to receive training as I treat-ed patients.

Pastor Jae-Yell Kim asked all of them to leave the room so the two of us could talk privately.

As if he had heard my prayer, or knew my weakness, he implored me, "Do not rely upon your knowledge or skills today. Rely entirely upon the Holy Spirit. Only He can heal these people."

When I heard that, I prayed and asked not for insight or skill but for the anointing of the Holy Spirit.

Chiropractic medicine requires few tools. All I needed was a treatment bed and my hands. That's the extent of the technology required in this field. Full of worry and anticipation, I prayed silently as I laid my hands on each patient I saw and treated them to the best of my ability.

I finished seeing the long line of patients and returned to my hotel room around 10:00 p.m. to complain to God. He had given me all older patients that chiropractic was not well suited to treat. He had given me an opportunity to treat patients in North Korea, but how could I treat these medical conditions in these physical conditions? The miracles of successful treatments and miraculous healings I had hoped for didn't happen.

I went to bed disappointed and discouraged.

The following day, our local guide came running to us, quickly urging us to come to the hospital because many patients were lining up waiting for me. I asked him if they were the same patients from yesterday. He got excited and explained that one grandfather who had come for treatment with foramen stenosis (a narrowing of the bones around the spinal cord, which resulted in severe leg and back pain) came back. Typically, people with this condition cannot walk for more than ten minutes at a time. But this man told our guide that he had walked for about an hour straight the day before, and as a result, he came back for treatment.

Another grandmother said that she had suffered from insomnia but after the treatment, she was able to sleep deeply for the first time.

God was truly fulfilling His promise. To be honest, I was so surprised.

After staying and treating patients for a month, rumors spread that many older people were getting healed, so more elderly people from all over the area came to the hospital to be treated.

One woman I will never forget came for treatment for adhesive capsulitis, a condition commonly referred to as "frozen shoulder." This "grandmother" (the general term used as a sign of respect for women over sixty) wore three or four layers of clothes, but her bony frame was still evident through her clothing. She had been unable to move her arms for seven years, unable to dress herself or perform daily household chores. In agonizing pain, she asked me to restore function to her arms. When I looked into her weathered face, I saw she resembled my own grandmother.

I prayed with all my heart for the Holy Spirit to heal this woman and alleviate her intense suffering. I knew that if I had all the modern medical equipment available for my use, it would take several months for her shoulders to improve. I honestly did not know if or how much she would improve through my simple chiropractic treatment.

However, God placed a special burden on my heart for this grandmother. That night I prayed earnestly for her, giving my medical skills and knowledge over to God and completely relying upon Him. My focus shifted from my own skills, and even any success in treatment, to glorifying the name of the Lord.

The next day she arrived in the afternoon for her second treatment session. As I laid my hands on her to do my work, I prayed and did my best to treat her. After the treatment, I suddenly found these words coming out of my mouth: "Grandma, raise your arms."

I myself was surprised at what I had said. However, as soon as the words came out, the grandmother slowly started to raise her arms. She lifted them higher and higher, all the way up to her shoulders.

The doctors surrounding me saw what was happening and started to shout, "What in the world? Her arms are going up. Her arms are moving! I can't believe it! Oh my! Unbelievable!"

A miracle was occurring right before my eyes. It was medically impossible to explain. I bet no one has ever seen a woman over sixty years old suffering from frozen shoulders for over seven years regain function in her arms after only two treatments!

The grandmother herself could not believe her eyes—or arms—as she practiced raising them up and down, ecstatic with joy. I felt awed, standing in the presence of the Lord and witnessing His power on display. I came to find out later that this woman was the mother of my guide, who had boldly asked me to treat patients as soon as we arrived.

That day changed my outlook forever. Up until then, I had promised to go to North Korea and give my life for the people, but I never really expected that God would be alive in North Korea. North Korea, as I thought about it, had always been a place full of darkness and sorrow. It was not a place we thought of where God's glory could appear. Why would it?

However, witnessing this grandmother's miraculous healing, I experienced the presence of the Living God. I saw His love for His creation. I saw His compassion for the suffering. I understood more profoundly what the moment when Jesus healed the woman from her bleeding would have been like for those there in the crowd (Mark 5:20).

There was no way that I could have done that in my own strength. I just had to be obedient and be present. God was the one who did the work. My role was to acknowledge the work of the Living God and praise Him for it.

From that day on, impossible things became possible. In place of tension and anxiety, a deep peace entered my heart. North Korea became a different place from what I knew the day before. Even the scenery felt new. Before, mountains in North Korea appeared bare, stripped of their trees. But from that moment on, the formerly shabby mountainside was transformed into a beautiful landscape of jagged peaks designed, created, and sustained by God.

That summer I treated hundreds of patients from 7:00 a.m. to 10:00 p.m. every day for an entire month. In these long and physically, emotionally, spiritually demanding days, God taught me to love people. As I treated patients, I also learned how to participate in both their pain and their joy. Most of all, I saw that God was alive in North Korea.

DECLARING HIS PRAISE

STEPHEN

*"I tell you," he replied, "if they keep
quiet, the stones will cry out."*

—LUKE 19:40

That summer a visitor from Pyongyang unexpectedly visited the hospital. From the window of the second-floor treatment room, I saw a black Mercedes drive up the hospital driveway. It was truly a rare sight in that city as there were few cars and certainly not any luxury vehicles in the region.

I could sense that something unusual was about to happen, as it appeared that a high-ranking officer from the capital city had arrived.

Immediately, all the doctor trainees were ordered out of my exam room, and a middle-aged man came in, supported, practically carried, by his subordinate. His head and back pains were so severe that he could not even stand on his own. While being treated in the city, he had heard about my work. Rumors of the grandmother miraculously being healed from frozen shoulder had spread throughout the city. He had come from Pyongyang to Rason to attend an important international conference being held there and came to see me for help.

The hospital's director told me who he was, but I could not hear anything because my heart was pounding so loudly. I was used to treating common villagers. Before me now was a high-ranking official. This man could make or break my life in North Korea.

The man was suffering from a severe headache and back pain. After taking a few deep breaths, I placed my hands on him and quietly prayed over him. Chiropractic adjustment lasted only about ten minutes. I asked him to get up. He jumped off the table and looked at me curiously.

"How could this be?" he wondered. "It's a miracle!"

He walked down the stairs on his own, without anyone's help. The attendants who had ushered him into the hospital looked at his recovery in disbelief.

The next day he had already made an almost full recovery, but he came for a second treatment anyway.

After I was done, he asked me in front of the room full of North Korean doctor trainees, "Doctor, you are from America. But are you Buddhist, or are you Christian?"

I wondered why he asked such a thing. "I am a Christian," I replied.

Then, suddenly, he began to recite John 3:16 in a deep Pyongyang dialect. "For God so loved the world that He gave his one and only Son, that whoever believes in Him shall not perish but have eternal life" (John 3:16).

I stood there shocked.

He looked at my surprised expression and explained that he had been a diplomat who had traveled to many countries around the world. I don't know if in his travels he had been exposed to the gospel or if it was diplomatic training that taught him this in order to engage with foreigners, but he turned to the North Korean doctors in the room and spoke with authority.

"Comrades, Doctor Yoon is a Christian. The Christian philosophy is to go into the world and share the love of God just as the Father gave His only Son to the world. Doctor Yoon came to our country with a heart to serve people, so you should learn well from Dr. Yoon."

As the official left, he told me to come to him whenever I needed help while working in North Korea. I didn't even say a single word, yet John 3:16 was shared with the doctors that day through this man. God revealed His glory in North Korea. The name of the Lord was exalted by a high-ranking North Korean official in the presence of those who had never heard the name of Jesus before.

Indeed, God can make even the rocks cry out His praise.

RAISED UP

STEPHEN

*Do not be afraid; keep on speaking, do
not be silent. For I am with you.*

—ACTS 18:9–10

While living in Rason, we wanted to experience the rest of the country, but there was no way to travel to other provinces from there. To travel to other regions, you first had to receive permission from the central government in Pyongyang. Permission was only granted by the capital city.

Our mentor, Pastor Peter Kim, traveled back and forth between Pyongyang and Rason often, and because of him, our team was given the opportunity to also visit Pyongyang.

Our whole family, including our children, went to the capital of North Korea for the first time with other team members, by way of Shenyang, China. Because of all the travel restrictions, it was actually easier to travel out to China and back into North Korea than to try to travel within the country. No direct flights there!

When we arrived in Pyongyang, it felt like we had entered a completely different world. There was a huge difference from rural Rason where we lived and worked. It was September, and every year, the Arirang Festival (a choreographed mass celebration involving thousands of people) was held. The games opened up an opportunity for foreigners from all around the world to visit the city.

I experienced a side of North Korea that I had never known existed before. Pyongyang was developed and organized. It portrayed the spirit and heart of the country much like Washington, DC celebrates the founding leaders of America. Like in DC, the streets were lined with flowering trees, and the city was designed intentionally to showcase the pride of the nation. As I was there, I saw that North Korea was a country with diversity, which included places like both Pyongyang and mountainous villages. I realized that I needed to be careful about thinking that since I had seen one region, then I had experienced the whole country.

The guide in charge of our trip was a middle-aged woman, and she took a special interest in our family. When I met her, I felt something special. She was polite and elegant, displaying the warmth of a mother.

As she accompanied us, she asked me questions here and there. She asked me what I did in Rason, what I thought about working there, why I had come to North Korea, and what purpose and goals I had for being there. These were rather sensitive questions, but I answered everything honestly. As a Christian, I simply explained that I went there because I wanted to go out into the world and share the love of Christ, and my American wife loved North Korea more than I did.

After hearing my story, she asked me to write it down for her. I wrote down my testimony of faith by hand in our hotel room. I honestly and openly documented my calling, receiving Jesus as my Savior, and even being commissioned as a cross-cultural worker by our church. If there was one thing that I had learned in North Korea, it was that I should never lie. Doing so could result in many consequences.

After a week of sightseeing, on the day of our departure, she asked me if I would like to come back and work in Pyongyang. She had been researching what I had been doing in Rason, and it turned out that rumors of my medical outreach in Rason had become known even in Pyongyang.

Our guide gave me detailed instructions on what to write in a letter to the government to request that I come back to Pyongyang to explore the possibilities of expanding our work there.

After a few weeks, I received a phone call from Pyongyang. This time I was asked to come to the capital city alone. When I arrived, our female guide as well as many other officials were there to greet me, and they immediately took me to a hospital in Pyongyang.

I wondered what in the world was going on. There were about fifteen North Korean doctors waiting for me. They explained my schedule to me. I would be taking medical examinations for eight days, eight hours a day. These tested me on my basic science, medical knowledge, pathology, as well as clinical performance. It was like taking a National Board exam.

Questions came pouring at me, and I had to answer them. In the afternoon, patients came in for treatment, but it turned out that many of them were doctors disguised as patients. The North Korean doctors were vetting me as a medical professional.

After intense examination, the doctors were convinced of my training in neurological and spine treatment. Since chiropractic treatment does not require expensive medical equipment, the doctors thought that this field would be a great asset to the North Korean medical system.

I was asked to start a medical program in Pyongyang to train doctors in this specialty.

It was difficult for me to provide an immediate answer to their request. It certainly was a good opportunity. Our family would relocate to the capital city, and we could potentially receive permission to expand our work into other parts of the country from there. However, I was aware that foreigners had opened hospitals before, and those projects ended up with the facilities being handed over to the government. By doing this, we could potentially lose our involvement in the projects and thus our ability to remain in the country at all.

What can guarantee that the same thing will not happen to me? I wondered.

As I discussed this concern with my female guide, she mentioned to me that it would be good if I could be officially recognized by the government, and one possible way for this to happen would be to earn a North Korean doctoral degree.

In North Korea, the only policies that cannot be changed or that are difficult to alter are those that are directly signed and implemented by the Party. The government is also the one that confers doctoral degrees, not academic institutions. Universities only grant degrees up to the master's level. PhDs are granted directly by the government and are viewed as a heroic status. I realized that if I were to obtain a North Korean doctorate degree, then I would be recognized as someone endorsed by the government and thus protected within the North Korean society.

To my surprise, through my guide, I received an official invitation.

"How would you like to earn a North Korean PhD in medicine?"

A medical degree from North Korea? It was an unexpected offer, to say the least. According to their terms, I would not receive an honorary degree; I would have to earn this degree on my own. Once I passed my dissertation defense and oral exam, I would be conferred the degree, but they would assign a research team to me to help carry out the necessary research for my doctoral dissertation. With North Korea being a socialist country, this whole process would be free of charge.

Our female guide also said that she would do everything to help me if I decided to go forward in this direction.

That evening, while I was praying in my hotel room, God gave me words from the book of Acts. "One night the Lord spoke to Paul in a vision: 'Do not be afraid; keep on speaking, do not be silent. For I am with you, and no one is going to attack and harm you, because I have many people in this city" (Acts 18:9–10).

God had opened this door, just as He had for me to study for a doctoral degree (D.C.) in America, and walking through it was an opportunity for me to demonstrate goodwill toward North Korea by doing well in this program.

That was exactly what I should do, I decided.

I wondered if God had possibly already sent me the people He was referring to in this passage.

He had.

From then on, I followed my North Korean counterparts, and our guide treated me as her own son. She had the guiding touch of a mother, a very nostalgic feeling for me after losing my mom as a teenager. I was greatly moved and comforted by her, and our friendship continues until today.

For the next two years, I went back and forth between Rason and Pyongyang to prepare for my dissertation with a research team from a local hospital. In April 2011, I became the first foreigner to obtain a medical doctorate degree in North Korea. I had come to North Korea to serve, but instead, God used my time there to raise me up. Much like Joseph who was sold as a slave and raised up to lead Egypt for the good of God's people, I was overwhelmed by God's ways.

When it came time for my graduation ceremony, I had to make a special request with the North Korean equivalents of the US State Department and Congress for Joy to be granted a visa and permission to attend the ceremony. I knew it wasn't an easy request by any means. The award ceremony was to be held at the

Mansudae Hall, which was the Korean National Assembly, and it was unprecedented for a white American to enter the building. But nonetheless, we received permission for her to attend.

A camera crew was waiting for us when we arrived at Pyongyang Airport. Everywhere we went, a photographer and film crew followed us. Questions from North Korean reporters poured in, and they interviewed me for a long time. It was like becoming a celebrity overnight.

My award ceremony was shown on the evening news. Everything seemed surreal.

After receiving my degree, my family moved to Pyongyang. We began living out of a hotel until we were granted permission to live in a home in a secure compound in the west part of the city. The following year, in 2012, I was appointed as a professor at the Pyongyang Medical University, and I was given an official position to clinically train doctors in the hospital and treat patients regularly.

Our team members in Rason continued running the factory and building kindergartens to serve the people in the countryside, and God began to use Joy and me to do amazing things in Pyongyang.

ORDAINED
OPPORTUNITY

JOY

*I will not leave you until I have done
what I have promised you.*

—GENESIS 28:15

As Stephen conducted research for his doctoral dissertation in Pyongyang, he made most of his trips into the city alone. The children and I were not allowed to accompany him, so we stayed behind in China where our team base was. When Stephen was ready to graduate and we requested permission for me to attend, we knew it was no small request. The ceremony was held in the Supreme People's Assembly, where the North Korean legislature met, a place where no white American had been granted access to before.

We were naturally somewhat skeptical of my chances. But the official permission came through! The three of us—Stephen, myself, and Stephen's father—would be attending the ceremony. We would then continue to stay for the celebrations of the founding leader's birthday.

The day of the ceremony arrived. Stephen prepared his "doctoral" speech in the hotel room that morning. I put on my traditional Korean dress for the ceremony. Our local guide went out and bought flowers as a congratulatory gift.

As we drove up to the National Assembly, a guard opened the gate for us and escorted us to the side entrance. TV news crews and newspaper reporters were waiting for us outside the room where the ceremony was to take place. The reporters interviewed Stephen for the newspaper, and the camera crews prepared to record the ceremony for the evening news. The departmental head for the board of education and the vice prime minister arrived to officiate the ceremony. Most of the researchers and doctors who were part of the doctoral thesis panel came to attend the ceremony also.

Doctors and officials lined up on the right side of the room. Stephen's father and I were placed on the left. The department head of the board of education stood in front next to the vice prime minister.

The vice prime minister announced to the crowd of doctors and scientists, "Stephen, please come forward to receive your degree," and Stephen stepped forward into the center of the room. "On behalf of the North Korean government, I hereby present to Stephen, a representative of Sunyang Hana, the award of doctorate in medicine. Congratulations!"

Stephen received his degree and shook hands with the vice prime minister. Then several doctors came forward to place a medal around Stephen's neck, and they pinned him with the doctoral star as the audience applauded.

My eyes teared up. *Is this really happening?* I thought.

During our first trip to Pyongyang, we had visited as a team just to scout it out, and I really sensed the Holy Spirit telling me that God had greater things in store for us in this city. Now I could see that God had kept that promise from two years prior. He was opening up new opportunities for us in North Korea, opportunities that were beyond our wildest imaginations.

Thoughts kept running through our minds: *Who are we to deserve such honor?*

God reminded us, *Be still and know that I am God.*

This was all His doing. We had not planned a single part of these events. To God be the glory!

All North Korean PhDs are approved by top government officials. North Korean officials went the extra mile to ensure my ability to attend the ceremony, so I felt that it was only fitting to write a thank-you note for the opportunity granted to us. I requested permission to write the letter.

From the beginning of our visit to Pyongyang for the graduation ceremony, I sensed a theme. Several officials discussed with me the significance of an American being invited into the National Assembly. Bitterness from the war still ran deep in the hearts of North Koreans. God was showing me the need for forgiveness.

I knew the atrocities of the war were vast—and that responsibility for them lies on both sides.

Most Americans could move on after the armistice, and the war barely affects our citizens now, but the pain from the war runs deep into North Korean society.

After Stephen's ceremony, we toured some orphanages and schools, as we often did, to see what the needs were and how we could help provide them. Visiting a school is also a way North Koreans practice hospitality. Foreign visitors are invited to tour the schools, and the students there will dance and perform music for them.

I saw that in schools they had pictures on the wall depicting war crimes committed by US soldiers. Although these pictures were used for propaganda, the effect kept the pain of the truth close at hand and top of mind. As a result, North Korea has lingering resentment and bitterness toward the United States.

Reconciliation is needed. Only humility and forgiveness would pave the way. Now God had opened the door for me to ask for reconciliation through the writing of my letter of thanks.

The Holy Spirit's presence overwhelmed me as I wrote the letter:

Thank you for the opportunity and incredible honor that you have given my husband by awarding him a North Korean doctoral degree. I understand that this was a huge act on the part of the North Korean government. I, especially, thank you for allowing me, an American citizen, to attend the ceremony.

While growing up in South Korea, I fell in love with the Korean people. Over the years, this love began to grow and extend to North Koreans as well. I have wholeheartedly supported the work my husband has done here in North Korea. Throughout our time working in North Korea, I have learned much about the country. After visiting local schools, I have seen pictures of the atrocities the US has inflicted upon the North Korean people. Upon learning this, I have wept bitterly for the pain we have caused this country.

I am just an ordinary citizen. I am nobody special. But as a US citizen, I would like to officially ask for your forgiveness for the pain America has caused this nation. My wish is that our countries would someday find reconciliation. And I thank you, from the bottom of my heart, for allowing me the opportunity to witness this special honor you have given my husband.

Though I wrote it in my best Korean, it undoubtedly had the subtleties that a foreigner brings to its language and structure, but we left it that way for authenticity's sake. When our guide read it, she laughed at first.

I was taken aback by that, but she explained, "This is so well-written, it took me by surprise. I give you a grade of 98 percent!"

Later I was told that she'd actually cried in response to the letter.

Upon reading it, another official held my hand tightly, with tears in his eyes, and thanked me.

Later, when we handed the letter to the official carrying it to governmental channels, he confessed to Stephen, "When I read this letter, I wept. I can see how much your wife loves Korean people. She is welcome in North Korea anytime."

I thank God for this ordained opportunity, and I pray that the road of reconciliation will continue to be paved in the hearts of both North and South Koreans—not just political reconciliation, but true reconciliation in the hearts of people. I believe that God will continue to work in that land to fulfill all the wonderful promises He has in store for the Korean people, and He will work in the hearts of Americans to break down the stereotypes and barriers that divide us instead of unite us. It is my prayer that Christians everywhere will see others through God's eyes, with the heart of the Father, and learn to love and accept others regardless of what our differences may be in race, gender, and political or economic ideologies.

IMMANUEL, GOD WITH US

JOY

And they will call him Immanuel
(which means "God with us").

—MATTHEW 1:23

The lack of a permanent home was one of the most difficult challenges for our family over the first few years. Constant traveling could be fun when you are single, or newly married, but trying to raise three children on the road was not easy, especially as we were constantly in a stage of transition. It was rare for our whole family to even be in one location for more than two to three weeks at a time. If Stephen wasn't in Pyongyang doing medical research, he was traveling abroad to raise funds for our projects.

The children and I lived in a rented apartment in China, but the landlady had decided to sell it. If she did, we would have to move for the fourth time since we arrived there about four years earlier. On top of that, our housing in North Korea was still in negotiation, and autumn was rapidly approaching, which didn't leave much time to build ourselves any foreign housing in Rason. It had been a two-and-a-half-year wait for Stephen's resident visa inside North Korea and another year and a half of waiting for my resident visa. After four years, we anticipated that we would be living full-time inside, but the time had not yet come.

During one of our visits inside, I walked among the village homes to a local corner market. A friend had taught me about the different vegetables planted in people's gardens. I talked with neighbors, and we began to build relationships. Our hearts longed even more now for the day of a consistent, long-term presence in the North Korean community.

Then, in 2011, as families around the world were gathering to celebrate the Christmas holidays, we were thrust into more upheaval when the media suddenly announced that the supreme leader of North Korea had died! This was a shock and yet also a very important time for the country. At the time, we did not know what changes his death and the assumption of the position by his third son might entail for the whole country or for our work. The entire country was in an official state of mourning, and governmental offices were officially closed.

Stephen was able to meet up with our company's workers inside and give them our sympathies, and we were surprised by an unexpected invitation for our family to go to the capital to pay our respects.

Due to the timing of this event, only Stephen and one co-worker could attend. They departed on Christmas Eve Day, December 24, and planned to be gone until at least December 27. It was difficult to have Stephen gone for Christmas, but we recognized the importance of this once-in-a-lifetime event. This invitation allowed him not only to pay his respects at the supreme leader's funeral but also to seize another opportunity to lift up the nation to our Father.

When Stephen and our teammate joined the line of mourners waiting to pay their respects, God impressed upon them the passage in Matthew 1:23, "'Behold, the virgin shall conceive and bear a son, and they shall call his name Immanuel' (which means God with us)." They celebrated the fact that though it was just the two of them there on Christmas Day, God was also there. As they stood in the frigid cold, waiting in line to pay their respects and standing with those who mourned, Stephen could feel that God was with him. Icy temperatures froze his limbs as they stood in the elements for hours that winter, but his heart was warmed by the presence of Immanuel.

Stephen planned to return on the twenty-seventh, but we received word from inside that the North Korean government was hoping for him to stay until the thirty-first. The Korean Overseas Compatriot Department had arranged for Stephen to participate in various funeral events and proceedings. It was a crucial time for our team to stand alongside our counterparts in North Korea.

The North Koreans received Stephen and our teammate so well that some exclaimed, "You really understand us, now you are really one of us."

The new chairman was an essential part of the funeral proceedings. As he came out to view the body, he shook the hands of the foreigners who had been invited. Stephen and our teammate were able to greet the new chairman himself!

Stephen and our co-worker arrived home safely on New Year's Day from their trip to the capital. Their trip was a vital time for building relationships through expressing our community's sympathies to the nation. But more than anything, God was reminding us that He is the One who goes before us, with us, and for us. Reminding us that in Jesus, He has also stood shoulder to shoulder with those who mourn.

That Christmas was not the first nor the last time our family was separated for the holidays. In place of the gift of family, God reminded us that the greatest gift He could ever give us is His presence. When God is with us, our cold and unemotional hearts can be transformed into hearts of warmth and embrace. Only by God going with us was this itinerant life of a sojourner, a life of instability, worth it. His presence made going through the ups and downs, all the uncertainties, possible. He was with us paving the way, transforming not only our lives but also the lives of those around us.

THE REAL BATTLE

STEPHEN

For our struggle is not against flesh and blood, but . . .
against the spiritual forces of evil in the heavenly realms.

—EPHESIANS 6:12

It was a fierce battle with invisible spiritual forces, not with people. If we are unaware of the spiritual battle playing out all around us, it is easy to waste time and energy on useless issues. I have firsthand experience with the spiritual forces of evil.

On December 17, 2011, the whole country was engulfed in deep sorrow because the State had lost its supreme leader. At that time, I was invited to participate in the funeral processions as a distinguished foreign guest. Former South Korean President Kim Dae-Jung's wife was also escorted to the funeral by bodyguards along with other significant VIPs. I attended the events alongside these significant figures.

On December 24, the day before Christmas, I arrived in Pyongyang. My team member and I held a Christmas worship service in our hotel room. I opened to the Gospel of Matthew and read from chapter one. Meditating on the Lord's coming, we prayed over the spiritual forces and strongholds in North Korea.

After the worship time in our hotel room, I looked out the window for a moment. Suddenly, I was surprised by what I saw. The room where we were in the Koryo Hotel was on the twentieth floor, and an object in the sky outside the building caught my eye. It was a dark abstract shape slowly gliding through the air. It wasn't human, just a form, but it seemed to bring with it a presence of evil and fear.

For me, it was my first experience with the dark side of the spiritual realm. Compared to this spiritual figure, I felt like a fly on the wall. I could feel its power and sensed it could kill me with one impulse if it chose to. This spiritual vision continued to manifest for several days. Wherever I went and whatever I did in the capital, I could feel the presence of this stronghold. It was evident in the atmosphere around me as well as in the responses I received from people, indicating the influence of these strongholds in people's hearts. This spiritual vision was another great turning point for me. I came to see firsthand that it is the spiritual forces of evil in the heavenly realms, not humans, that are holding North Korea (Ephesians 6:12).

When I got home, I told Joy that I had to go to South Korea right away. I went to see Rev. Park, my spiritual mentor, thinking that I should share with him the vision that I saw. After hearing my story, Rev. Park said that he felt like we needed more people to pray with us. I had trouble sleeping after my experience with spiritual darkness, and consequently, I met many people and visited many churches, sharing and praying with others for two weeks straight.

However, while I was in South Korea, I realized that the same spirit I saw in North Korea had also entered the South Korean church. Though I could not see a spirit floating in the air, I could see the spirit of idolatry was there too, as well as the spirit of pride, unforgiveness, division, fear, and secularism. I was shocked to see all the evil spirits from North Korea in the South Korean church.

In my heart and mind, the Holy Spirit was showing me that in order for these strongholds to be broken down, my paradigm needed to shift. The division on the Korean Peninsula could only be combated with unity, including cooperation with the Korean church. It shifted my thinking, and I began to understand that North Korea would change as cooperation with the Korean church increased. It is not just that North Korea should change but that South Korean churches must also repent in order for them to be restored together. Recognizing that this dark spirit was dominating us, our community realized that the entire Korean Peninsula must be transformed for the image of Christ to be thoroughly revealed. This was not a task for one person. It would require all of us.

There is no doubt that these spiritual strongholds exist not only in North Korea but in every nation because we have all sinned and allowed Satan to gain a foothold. Each country may have different strongholds because strongholds come from corporate sin. But when it comes to the strongholds that are captivating the Korean Peninsula, there are similar strongholds that I see in America.

As I prayed, I realized even more that God's anointing would be necessary to tear down the spiritual strongholds holding captive the Korean Peninsula. Without knowing it, our team had become less compassionate and more authoritative in our interactions with North Koreans. Through this spiritual experience, I was deeply awakened to the sanctifying work of Christ and the fruit of the Holy Spirit.

I realized that the only way to combat these spiritual strongholds was to surrender myself more to the sanctifying work of the Holy Spirit. I needed to walk in the opposite spirit to these strongholds. Where there was fear, I chose to walk in God's perfect love. Where there was pride, I desired to follow in Christ's humility. Where there was idolatry, I intentionally worshipped our one and only God. The more intense the spiritual warfare, the more Christ's character should be revealed through us.

Satan blinds and binds people away from God, and I discovered that the way to approach this spiritual battle was by living and walking in opposition to these spirits. For example, to oppose the spirit of idolatry, we are to live a life of worship in spirit and truth. In other words, where there is true worship, the spirit of idolatry will disappear. When we are thoroughly united with our brothers and sisters in Christ and those around us, the spirit of division will disappear.

The way to counter the spirit of pride is to walk in humility. When we walk in humility, the stronghold weakens, and Christ's likeness and glory are revealed, attracting people to Christ.

Through the course of our work since then, we've found that confronting the spiritual battle with the godly spirit proves to be a wiser strategy than confronting the battle head-on.

Once, in 2012, our team visited Pyongyang after being invited to a commemorative event being held there. Many domestic and foreign teams attended, and during our stay there, we operated with intentional love and humility. After the event, our team voluntarily picked up the trash that was thrown on the ground, and our team members naturally ran to help and support the elderly people we met throughout the event (a cultural sign of respect).

At the end of our visit to Pyongyang, a North Korean official came to our team and told us that we had been the most courteous, kind, and respectful team they had hosted. He said that he could see how our team was united in one accord. We did not intentionally demonstrate this to garner praise or commendation. We weren't asking for compliments, and we did not talk about our identity as Christians. It was just that the love we had for North Korea flowed naturally from our hearts. God had revealed Himself to this man through us.

Where the glory of God abides, darkness automatically retreats, because light and darkness cannot coexist. When Christ's love is revealed to people, the spiritual strongholds of North Korea disappear. Therefore, our job is to approach the strongholds in the opposite spirit. We are to bless the country with forgiveness and love and with a spirit of humility and trust. Then the glory of God will turn the darkness into light. God will heal and restore both South and North Korea, the entire peninsula of Korea.

Our wrestling is never against flesh and blood, but it is against the evil spirits and powers in the heavenly realms (Ephesians 6:12). We must never forget what it is that we are fighting against.

LEARNING TO LOVE
EACH OTHER

J O Y

And over all these virtues put on love, which
binds them all together in perfect unity.

—COLOSSIANS 3:14

After six years of waiting, traveling back and forth, and temporary hotel living, our family was finally able to live inside North Korea! It was a dream come true. But as most dreams go, the reality of it was quite different from what we had imagined. There was no comfortable personal home to live in. Instead, our whole team had to share one house together. Usually, that meant the five of us in our family, plus one single man and two single ladies; but other times, when we hosted guests or other team members, we could have up to fifteen people living there.

At first, it was beyond our wildest expectations. We were permitted to live in a large home that was constructed around 1980 to host presidents from various communist countries when the communist nations came together for conferences in North Korea. The home had four bedrooms: one for the two of us, one for our three children, one for men, and one for women. Each bedroom had its own private bathroom, but we shared the common living space and kitchen. We had never imagined such luxury, nor could we have anticipated the beautiful landscape that surrounded us. We had a small corner of the garden, which was a great source of refreshment to me, though we were restricted from roaming completely freely within it because it was guarded by the military 24-7.

But just as in the Garden of Eden, the beauty of this garden was shattered by the realities of living life closely together with other people. The challenges of community life infringed upon our beautiful little garden and the peace in our home. The housing we received as a team went from being a gift of joy to a prison cell, confining us all to a community lifestyle that none of us were prepared for.

Laundry had to be done by hand. I did my family's, and the other adults did theirs. Most of the time, there was no hot water. At times there was no running water at all. The kitchen became a battle zone. Now that we were all living together, and there was only one kitchen, we decided to eat all our meals together (attempting to be a model Asian community). At first, the women bore most of the burden as we cooked and cleaned up for our team of ten people. But the work of cooking three meals a day, every day, for ten people began to drag us down. Unlike in a home with a family where the culture formed around the family's needs or preferences, these were all adults who brought with them their own preferences, cooking styles, and eating habits.

Instead of turning to one another for help and comfort, each person ended up withdrawing into our own caves, becoming reclusive from the team. In the end, what resulted was only a few dedicated team members carrying out the daily tasks of waking up early in the morning, preparing breakfast, packing lunches for the whole team, tediously cleaning the kitchen, and preparing the main evening meal for everyone.

In the beginning, all we had were mini refrigerators to store our food, which would have been sufficient if it were not for the fact that we could only go to the market once a week. All the groceries for ten to fifteen people had to be bought a week at a time, and we had very little space to keep them fresh. The only market open to foreigners was a half-hour drive away and was only open certain hours during the week. We bought everything in bulk, hoping that the produce would stay fresh until next week's market run. Eggs had to be checked to see if they were rotten. Rice had to be sifted every day to remove rocks. Meat had to be skinned, gutted, and cut once we got home. It did not come wrapped in plastic on a styrofoam tray. The regular activities of daily life were a full-time job and became a test of endurance.

On top of this was the stress of our children's boredom and loneliness. Homeschooling had been our only option for educating them. Not only were foreigners forbidden from attending public schools, but if our kids had been allowed there, they would have been taught North Korean and communist ideology. So we continued homeschooling in our new home, but because the children did not attend school, there was little opportunity for them to leave the little garden compound in which we lived. No other children lived within the compound, so there were no friends for our kids to play with.

Through another Christian family, we discovered the Pyongyang Korean School for Foreigners. We thought it might be worth investigating to see if it would be a possibility for our children. We could see that our children needed a social outlet. Going to school would help them not only adjust to living inside North Korea but also give them routine and stability, which would allow us to stay inside for longer periods of time. Once we visited the school, we made the decision to enroll them.

Now the entire team would depart from our house early in the morning, and the kids would go to school. On our way to the hospital, we would drop the kids off at school. Slowly, our team started adjusting to the new routine, new work, and new life together as a one-home community. What kept us sane and knitted us together was our regular team prayer and worship times. The Spirit of the Lord brought healing and restoration to our broken and tired souls. We discovered that there is unity in the presence of the Holy Spirit. Soon all our petty grievances and problems among each other seemed insignificant in light of what God was doing.

We realized that in order for us to live in community, we had to love one another. Christ commanded us as his disciples to "love one another." *Love* is more than a word. Love is an action. We must sincerely demonstrate our love for one another. Sincere love is patient and endures all things. Ultimately, love is sacrifice. Love does not stand by and watch. It acts. Just as Christ sacrificed all, to the point of death for our salvation, we are called to sacrifice in love.

We were learning to clothe ourselves in love for one another within our team and therefore demonstrate Christ's love to those around us. We were called to be a living example of a Christian community and the body of Christ. And through love, we would find perfect harmony.

THE GIFT OF BLESSING

STEPHEN

Unless a kernel of wheat falls to the ground and dies, it remains a single seed. But if it dies, it produces many seeds."

—JOHN 12:24

The first time I met Blessing was in Rason. An elderly woman carrying a child tied on her back came into our cold, stoveless clinic. She said that her granddaughter was very sick, and she untied the little girl and laid her on my table. This small four-year-old girl suffered from severe spastic quadriplegic cerebral palsy. She was unable to move a single finger. I could see that her mouth was frozen open and her head was turned to one side. She couldn't chew food, so her grandmother would chew her food for her and then spoon it into her mouth.

I looked intently at this little girl. I could feel God's love and compassion for this child. This overwhelming love gave me the sense that she was my own daughter. At that time, my youngest daughter was also about four years old, giving me even more compassion for Blessing. How much she must have suffered being born in this disabled body. As I gazed upon Blessing, I repeated these words, "My daughter, my daughter."

As rumors spread about a foreign doctor being in town, seriously ill patients came from all over the region, but it was the first time that I would treat a child with severe cerebral palsy. Because of that also, I had a special attachment to this child.

I did the best I could and worked hard to treat her. After a few weeks of treatment, her muscle movements began to change. She was able to move her fingers and clench her fists. Her expression became much more comfortable than it was at first. Watching her improve inspired me even more. I wanted to serve her better, so I studied all night before her treatments. What I did not know, I learned from experts in South Korea as I made trips back and forth. I was both amazed and thankful that Blessing was improving.

However, a few months later, I was appointed as a professor of the Rehabilitation Medicine Department at KIM-IL SUNG University's Pyongyang Medical School, and our family relocated to Pyongyang. The one thing that bothered me about our move was leaving Blessing behind. I was worried that there would be no one left to care for this child in my absence.

As soon as I arrived in Pyongyang, I asked the director of the Pyongyang Medical School Hospital to prepare a bed for Blessing so that she could continue to receive treatment. In response, the director asked me how I had come to treat a child with cerebral palsy when there were no children with cerebral palsy in North Korea. I knew for a fact that there were, but I didn't dare argue with him. I simply explained that I had been treating this child in Rason, so I earnestly requested for her to be transferred to Pyongyang.

Thankfully, the director gave me one inpatient bed for Blessing. Blessing's bed was in a room with eight other children in the children's ward of the Pyongyang Medical School Hospital. Each inpatient room is about the size of four square meters, not technically large enough to hold eight beds. Although the environment was poor, I was grateful to have the opportunity to continue treating Blessing. I immediately made the arrangements for Blessing to make the long trip to Pyongyang and resume treatment.

After six months, Blessing's grandmother came to me and said that she was planning on taking a break from treatment and taking Blessing home. I asked her why she had a sudden change of heart. The grandmother hesitated, not wanting to answer my question. But then she confessed that it was just too difficult for her to live in the hospital for such a long period of time. The other seven patients that Blessing shared a room with were uncomfortable watching this grandmother chew Blessing's food for her and change her diapers in the narrow ward they lived in. Regardless of who they were rooming with, we were likely to receive similar complaints, and it was not possible for us to find a private inpatient room for Blessing.

As is the case around the world, patients in the hospital are expected to be discharged as quickly as they can be from the hospital to make space for other patients. Other children were waiting in line to be treated, and Blessing had already taken up a bed for six long months. Her grandmother must have felt the pressure to be discharged when she heard that other children were not receiving hospital benefits because her granddaughter was taking too long to be healed. I tried to convince her to stay, but in the end, Blessing and her grandmother left to return home.

On the day they were discharged, Blessing's grandmother begged me to make a hospital where children like Blessing could stay comfortably for as long as they needed. Her wish became my earnest desire, but at that time, I could not make any promises to her. All I could say to her was to rest well during their break and to return for treatment as soon as possible. Upon return, I would do my best to prepare a better room for them.

Children like Blessing had never before been treated in the hospital as their condition was considered to be incurable. All the people in the hospital had watched Blessing being treated for her cerebral palsy and regain function. However, after Blessing returned home, something unexpected happened. People who had seen this happen for Blessing told other people who had children with cerebral palsy that if they just brought their child to the hospital, their child could be helped.

After the word got out, families with children who had cerebral palsy from all over the country began to flock to my treatment room. A long line of parents and their children lined up. Upon seeing this, the director of the hospital realized that he had to do something. We were in the middle of discussing the establishment of a spine rehabilitation center with the Pyongyang Medical School Hospital to treat patients with nonsurgical spine care. However, after Blessing's departure, we decided to also establish a hospital specializing in pediatric developmental and behavioral disorders. By changing the structure of the rehabilitation center, an additional ward could be used for inpatient rooms for children with severe cerebral palsy like Blessing. All this gave us new hope for bringing Blessing back for treatment in Pyongyang.

Blessing stayed home for about a full year. While she was gone, several children walked out of the hospital on their own, and many children experienced improvement in amazing ways. I wished that Blessing would return as soon as possible, so I asked a team member near Rason to meet Blessing's parents and convey my wishes for her to return for treatment.

A few days later, I got a call from Rason. Our team member had met Blessing's father and explained to him that children like Blessing were experiencing incredible transformation and were walking out of the Pyongyang Medical School Hospital, so he should bring Blessing back to Pyongyang quickly.

With tears in his eyes, Blessing's father responded, "What should I do? Blessing is no longer with us."

When I heard these words on the phone, I was so shocked that I couldn't respond at all. After hanging up the phone, I cried out loud for some time. She was like my daughter, and I had waited so long for her to return. I never dreamed that I would never see her again.

Because of Blessing, surprising things began to happen in North Korea, things never before thought possible, and now it was heartbreaking to know that Blessing was gone.

From that day on, I decided to prioritize our work for children like Blessing. When I think of Blessing, I feel indebted to her. I am determined to create a better future for other children like her. I want to give them hope, to encourage parents who sacrificially raise children with disabilities in North Korea.

I thought the day would come when Blessing would get better. I wanted to give that gift to Blessing. But instead, Blessing gave us one of the greatest gifts of all. She opened the door for us to serve an entire nation of children like her. We do not have statistics for how many people are diagnosed with cerebral palsy in North Korea, but according to the Centers for Disease Control and Prevention, worldwide approximately 3.3 out of every 1,000 children are affected by cerebral palsy. Based on the 2008 DPRK census, we can estimate that there are possibly 18,000 children with cerebral palsy in North Korea who need treatment.

Children with disabilities should not be thought of as a burden. It is the privilege to serve the weakest of the weak in the world. They give us a heart to look out for our neighbors, to share the goodness from within us. Each person is a precious blessing from God.

Blessing is no longer on this earth, but thanks to Blessing, children with cerebral palsy in North Korea are able to find hope and a future. Potential treatment centers in each province of North Korea have been approved by the Ministry of Public Health, and graduate training programs for medical specialists have also been approved by North Korea's medical education system. Because of Blessing, an opportunity for new life came to countless children who had been hidden behind doors.

One day, when I possibly meet Blessing in heaven, I want to be able to proudly tell her that I finished my race well. I want to honestly be able to say that I obeyed the command to love my neighbor as myself, to love the weak and the marginalized.

26

WHEN CHILDREN CAN DREAM

STEPHEN

"For I know the plans I have for you," declares the Lord, "plans to prosper you and not to harm you, plans to give you hope and a future."

—JEREMIAH 29:11

Ten-year-old Olivia lived in a rural district near Pyongyang. She had cerebral palsy, and since she was quadriplegic, she could not stand up on her own and was primarily confined to the house. Her schoolteacher felt pity for Olivia, so the teacher voluntarily carried her on her back to school every morning. She simply wanted to give Olivia the same opportunity to learn just like any other child. Since there were no special desks for children with disabilities, Olivia's teacher would strap her to a chair so that she could remain seated upright throughout the class's lessons. Her teacher cared for Olivia in this way for two years, feeding her lunch and carrying her home after class.

With this kind of love and courage, Olivia's teacher finally took her into the city and to my hospital for treatment. Olivia deserved help and a second chance in life, she reasoned. When I met Olivia, her joints moved a little, but her arms and legs moved in a completely uncoordinated way. Olivia and I gazed into each other's eyes and decided to make a joint effort to help her reclaim physical function.

From that day on, I found myself tirelessly striving to treat Olivia. Cerebral palsy is a disability that has many variations in how it manifests in the patient's body. Each individual's diagnosis is the same, but their physical symptoms and limitations can vary widely. Each child requires a creative approach to discover what triggers the condition and how to help improve it. Because of this, all that occupied my thoughts when I woke up in the morning was how to effectively treat my patients. In addition to providing a loving hand full of hope, I also wanted to impart God's touch upon these children's lives.

Rehabilitation therapy was not an easy process for Olivia. Her arms and legs would not cooperate as desired, and she often burst into tears from the frustration and discouragement with the slow, difficult treatments that required so much effort from her. Olivia's dream was to one day walk to school alongside her other classmates. In order to achieve this simple dream, she endured the pain of daily rehabilitation. Olivia also underwent two surgeries to stretch her stiffened ligaments.

After one year of treatment, Olivia miraculously walked out of the hospital. North Korea's broadcasting company came to cover her story, detailing the success of her treatment, and a documentary of her story was broadcast all over the nation. Olivia's story became famous across North Korea. Through this documentary, it became apparent to me that North Korea was changing. Children with disabilities who had once been hidden at home and not acknowledged were now being recognized. Realizing the potential that children with disabilities still had, Pyongyang Medical School Hospital started working in earnest to treat children with cerebral palsy.

When Olivia was leaving the hospital, I asked her a question. I remembered what she had told me one year ago. Now that her wish to walk to school with her friends was coming true, I asked her what her new dream was. Olivia turned to look directly into my eyes and said, "My dream is to become a doctor like you so that I can treat children like me."

At these unexpected words, tears began to run down my cheeks. Others listening to our conversation also began to tear up at Olivia's statement. I was deeply touched that a child with cerebral palsy was starting to dream about the possibilities for her future. She offered comfort and encouragement for me to continue to strive toward serving children with disabilities.

Olivia returned to school. This time instead of being carried to school on her teacher's back, she walked to school with her friends. I am so thankful for the teacher who sacrificed so much for her student. I am grateful for her love and courage that never gave up on Olivia by bringing her to our hospital for treatment. It was inspiring to witness such a passionate teacher here on earth. I want children like Olivia to know that they are not alone. There is someone fighting for them and cheering them on. Any burden too heavy to carry becomes lighter when it is shared, just like Olivia's teacher carried her on her back for two whole years.

Later a child named Ian from Hamgyeong Province came and knocked on the door of my clinic. Ian could not speak well or walk properly, but he greeted us with playful eyes. While receiving treatment for four years, he started to learn English from my wife, Joy. As Joy provided education for children with cerebral palsy, his speaking ability improved rapidly. Ian is incredibly bright and has perfect pitch, and once he hears a song, he can immediately sing it back, note for note.

One day he stuck his head through the door of the treatment room beaming ear to ear with a radiant smile and out of the blue asked me to ask him what his dream was. As Ian looked at me, I asked him what his dream was. This little boy's answer caused the clinic to rumble in excitement.

"My dream is to become a diplomat. I want to be a foreign diplomat!"

No words could describe how lovely Ian looked when he answered so confidently.

I was filled with joy that Olivia and Ian were now able to dream. I wanted to hold their hands and support them so that these children could face a new future. Dreams that seemed impossible came true by working together, and now they could dream even bigger.

Imagine the day that Olivia would come back to our hospital as a doctor to treat other children just like her. Olivia would give back abundantly more than what we'd given her. Just like Olivia, I envision Ian traveling around the world as a diplomat. Ian too would one day help other children achieve their dreams. This is the beauty of God's miraculous work. To Him be the glory!

27

ENLARGING OUR VISION

JOY

Enlarge the place of your tent, stretch your tent curtains wide, do not hold back . . . For you will spread out to the right and to the left . . .

—ISAIAH 54:2-3

When our children started to attend the Pyongyang Korean School for Foreigners on the embassy compound, I no longer spent my mornings homeschooling and ended up with free time. I was able to start accompanying the team to the Pyongyang Medical School Hospital. As I watched children with cerebral palsy being treated in the hospital, I realized something surprising. The children with disabilities receiving therapy were often past the age of going to school, yet many of them had never received an education. Knowing that, I immediately took it upon myself to advocate for the education of these children.

Little by little, I started talking to the hospital staff about the importance of providing educational opportunities for children with disabilities. With training and experience as a teacher and homeschooling my own children, I had enough foundation as an educator to advocate for this.

In this way, each child who came for treatment also started an individualized education program. We began to see remarkable changes in their bodies and their minds. A ten-year-old girl with cerebral palsy learned to read and write. A nine-year-old boy discovered his incredible ability to hear music and mimic notes on the piano. A seventeen-year-old had a speech impairment and was unable to communicate with people around him. But through many hours of speech therapy, this student also became more confident in speaking and in developing interpersonal relationships.

As each child began to change and develop through their specialized education, special education for children with behavioral and developmental disabilities was established in North Korea for the first time. I directed special educational programs for pediatric patients in the Pyongyang Medical School Hospital. Together with the hospital staff, we developed special educational courses for these children who had never before been to school due to their cerebral palsy, autism, or other learning challenges.

As a special educator, I taught math, science, English, and even Korean to North Korean children. To think about an American teaching Korean to North Korean children is laughable! I, being a white American, was the epitome of their enemy. Yet now I taught their own language to their children!

Children with cerebral palsy in the hospital began partic-
ipating in therapy in the morning and then special education
in the afternoon. For the first time, these children were valued
as being worthy of receiving an education. Many of them were
eager to learn. Others struggled with their learning challenges.
But each and every one of the children showed significant progress in their development.

This motivated parents to keep their children in therapy.
Before including special education as part of our therapeutic
program, it was easy for parents to lose hope. Therapy took
months, if not years, to see substantial results. But if consistent over time, those children could make tremendous strides.
Adding educational therapy to these patients' daily routines
provided more immediate results and small wins worth celebrating. Parents began to see not only the physical progress
of their children but also their cognitive, social, and academic
development. One parent even confessed to us that she remained
in the hospital for her child's treatment for this exact purpose.
The longer each child received daily therapy, the more they improved functionally in all areas.

The transformation of the children I worked with in the
hospital is best described by the words of Olivia, whom Stephen
wrote about in the last chapter. Toward the end of her stay in
the hospital, Olivia wrote a poem (which I have translated here)
describing her life transformation:

A seed was sown
Amongst the rocks.
The tree had a wish,

But the seed could not know
Whether it was a tree or not.
Either for the next generation
Or for the goal of reproduction,
The tree produced forth fruit,
And a seed was sown.
But why is the wind so strong?
In the midst of turbulence
Flying in a whirlwind,
The tree had a wish:
To plant the seed in fertile soil . . .

The seed in this poem represents Olivia's life. Her parents are the trees. But her life was so difficult that she did not know if she would ever grow up and develop into a tree. Through treatment, Olivia was finally planted in fertile soil. She now had a nurturing environment in which she could grow and flourish.

God was also expanding our horizons. We were bursting at the seams with the work that God had entrusted us with. It was almost more than we could handle. But we trusted that as we stretched ourselves to embrace that which God had given us, He would give hope to many lives and allow descendants of the next generation to flourish and bless the land.

BUILDING HOPE
FOR CHILDREN

STEPHEN

The Lord himself goes before you and will be with
you; he will never leave you nor forsake you.

—DEUTERONOMY 31:8

In South Korea, up until the 1970s or 80s, when children were born with disabilities, most were kept hidden at home. This similar social atmosphere was made clear to us in North Korea while treating Blessing. Children born with behavioral and developmental disorders such as cerebral palsy had few opportunities to receive a proper diagnosis or treatment. Even doctors at the hospital displayed similar attitudes when children were born with or showed these kinds of symptoms. It's difficult enough for able-bodied people to thrive, so doctors often told parents not to let their child suffer needlessly but to let their child die quickly. In North Korea, most children who came to the hospital with disabilities were sent home in this manner. Children with disabilities often ended up spending much of their time at home and alone, causing their conditions to worsen.

Treatment requires a lot of time and effort, and even so, usually, a child will have to live with some aspect of his or her disability for the rest of their life. We must do everything we can to help these children.

When Blessing passed away, I made a commitment to empower the dreams of children like her and Olivia. If children with cerebral palsy received timely treatment, the number of children who could participate in society and lead independent lives would significantly increase.

Although there were success stories, like Olivia, who walked out of the hospital on their own, there were also many children whose parents stopped treatment and took them home without significant improvement because of their various circumstances and limitations. I don't know what happened to each of them, but from time to time, we did hear of some who had passed away.

Every time I heard news like this, my heart ached, and I struggled to continue.

The reality of the situation that I faced was to treat severely disabled children every day with only a few, limited instruments, modalities, or implements in a treatment room measuring about five feet by four feet.

All the children who returned home after waiting for their turn to receive treatment haunted my thoughts. I was determined to build an adequate hospital so that no other children would have to give up on treatment because there was no room for them. As a result, the Pyongyang Medical School Hospital's Spine and Pediatric Behavioral and Developmental Disorder Treatment and Research Institute was born, but we call it the Spine Rehabilitation Center for brevity's sake.

Since most of the treatment I provided in North Korea up until that point was spine-related, my initial desire was to build a hospital for nonsurgical spine care. However, after meeting children with disabilities in North Korea, a specialized hospital for children with behavioral and developmental disorders, including cerebral palsy and autism, was established. Pyongyang Medical School and I were now working together to treat both spine patients and children with cerebral palsy.

As it stands, the Spine Rehabilitation Center is the largest pediatric rehabilitation center in North Korea. It can accommodate about 450 outpatients per day and 40 inpatients, including their guardians. The building itself is five stories high, in addition to a basement. Considering the difficulties children with disabilities and their caregivers have living in the hospital, we intentionally designed and equipped the facility to make hospitalization a pleasant experience.

Construction began in the summer of 2013, and originally, it was a $200,000 project, but as the hope for whom to treat expanded, so did the plans and budget. In the end, it cost about $4 million.

Construction projects are challenging anywhere, but in North Korea, they are exceptionally hard due to a lack of resources and intermittent electricity. Among the challenges we faced was a changing political climate that arose due to sanctions placed against North Korea.

In 2016, President Obama's administration designated North Korea as a money-laundering nation, and the political climate shifted to the point that it was necessary to prove that the finances used for the hospital did not support a terrorist state. In other words, our project had to be approved by the US Treasury Department for funds to go toward a hospital being built purely for humanitarian purposes. Because of this, I had to go to Washington, DC, and find a way to explain our project to governmental officials such as the State Department, the Ministry of Finance, and the Ministry of Commerce.

Even though our project was purely medical in nature, we had to go through the process of applying for and receiving approvals from the United Nations and each of these departments within the US government.

My time was still insufficient to treat all the children who needed help in North Korea, and now I had to spend much of it navigating the bureaucracy of the US government instead of providing care. The only thing that motivated me was remembering the faces of my patients. If only I could save the lives of these children, I was willing to take on anything, even governmental red tape. I promised God that I would convey His heart for these children to those around me. God never gives up on His children.

But something else really bothered me. At that time, there were people who opposed the establishment of the hospital because of the international political situation surrounding North

Korea. They argued that it was not the right time to do a project like this. Even those willing to move forward with the project said that they would support it once the political situation improved. I always contrasted this perspective with one question.

"If that is so, then when would be the best time? Should it be after more children have lost their lives?"

Speaking from my vantage point on the front lines of meeting their needs, I just couldn't stand by and watch children die without giving them a chance at a new life. There is no wrong time for saving lives.

From that moment on, our work to save the children of North Korea became all-consuming. I had no choice but to fight for them because it was literally a matter of life and death—theirs. The lives of these children and the hope and despair of their parents depended upon how much I shared in their pain.

It hurt my heart to realize that a suffering child could be given a future but that we had to wait because of political tensions outside our control. Seeing children die in these circumstances, I asked God why.

There were many unanswered questions I battled with during this time. I was upset about the situation within North Korea, and on other days, I was angry about the political tension toward North Korea from without.

What really upset me was the root of bitterness in my own heart. My heart ached at the cynical responses behind lukewarm receptions from churches where I shared about our work. As the hands and feet of Jesus who believes all humans are made in God's image, the church, of all people, should readily help children with disabilities. "To whom much is given, much is required," and their lack of concern and compassion frustrated me.

How could I make them see that this wasn't a political issue but a human issue? Children with disabilities in North Korea were forced to overcome not only their physical and mental limitations but also the political and social environment.

It was difficult to observe that the church itself seemed to place a higher value on political ideologies than on alleviating human suffering and restoring human dignity. The church hesitated to follow Jesus because of politics and economics. Satan was keeping us from living out the gospel!

I began to share Blessing's and Olivia's stories with churches as a way to communicate the need from a personal perspective. The sacrifice and service of Olivia's teacher, Blessing's grandmother's devotion and tender care, and the hardship of life and difficulty of obtaining and sustaining treatment for her struck a chord. Her story was able to affect people's hard hearts. Even though Blessing's story was tragic, it created opportunities for people to hear about the need and help, and for others like her to be treated.

Soon, even in the most challenging political situations, churches and individuals began to give strength and support to this hospital and to the treatment of children with cerebral palsy. Countless people of faith laid down their own political inclinations and leaned into the Lord's heart to serve the "least of these." I began to believe again that yes, the One who began a good work in us will indeed complete it to the end.

In spite of a nearly impossible international climate and difficult circumstances, little by little, the hospital building rose higher and higher. Year after year, construction slowly carried on. After seven years of what could have been done in five or six months in another country, everyone, both the North Koreans and the Christian community, was astonished that the hospital's construction was finally finished.

In addition, an agreement with the North Korean Ministry of Public Health was signed, and I became the official co-director of the hospital, allowing me to ensure the successful running of hospital operations.

My hope is that this hospital will not just be a building. Our true hope is for this hospital to break down the barriers between people and give opportunities for broken relationships to reconnect and heal. Despite differing social and political environments, our hope is for this to become a place where people can meet together with a heart of helping those who are weaker than themselves. A church of sorts.

Now no doctor in the hospital tells parents to give up and let the child die quickly. Rather, they have joined their hearts with ours to do their best in treating children with disabilities. Hospitals like this need to be built all throughout North Korea. This can only be accomplished by paving a way with God's love.

CALLED,
NOT QUALIFIED

STEPHEN

Blessed are the poor in spirit, for theirs
is the kingdom of heaven.

—MATTHEW 5:3

"Aren't they just building a hospital?" North Koreans thought. When they first saw us in Pyongyang, they just thought of us as the people who came to construct a hospital. Of course, there are still people who only see us this way. Most NGOs in North Korea work on behalf of children, medicine, and agriculture. Many have contributed to the building of hospitals or importing medicine, so it's not totally unfair of them to think of us that way, though our work is more expansive than that.

We needed an adequate hospital, but our goal wasn't just to provide a medical facility. What was really important was providing treatment to suffering children and delivering medical technology not yet introduced in the nation. Fortunately, as we worked and lived together in Pyongyang, North Koreans began to understand our intentions little by little. We joined efforts to treat patients, impart technology and treatment methodologies to doctors, and create a medical system for children with disabilities.

To them, I was a foreigner. There were others who wondered why we didn't just build the hospital and leave.

What were these foreigners sticking around for? they thought.

Perhaps our presence caused them a lot of inconvenience. We kept advocating for the needs of children with disabilities, but to them, it might have sounded like interference or nagging.

If I had just tried to persuade North Koreans to help children, it would have not worked, but because this project came about naturally in response to a need, our North Korean counterparts were more agreeable with the values we insisted upon. God's leading is often confirmed when we see Him accomplish things that we cannot do on our own. I was determined that if I must do something in North Korea, it should be something that saves lives in the country. By putting lives first, this surprising work brought about unexpected changes in North Korea.

Until we moved to Pyongyang, there was no official treatment or education for children with behavioral and developmental disorders such as cerebral palsy or autism. It was impossible to find a single specialist in this field. Hospital administrators and government officials had a hard time admitting that there were even such children in their country. Although there were a few paragraphs introducing developmental disorders in their medical textbooks, their medical education did not include any treatment or academic study for these disabilities. Through Blessing, cerebral palsy came into the mainstream view for the first time, and this opportunity opened up an official way to address these disorders.

Thousands of children are now waiting for treatment in North Korea. Cerebral palsy was officially registered as a condition at the Pyongyang Medical School Hospital, and hospitalization for this condition was made possible for the first time ever. In addition, specialty courses in therapeutic treatment for cerebral palsy were added to the medical school course selection. Graduates who complete these specialized courses are dispatched to provincial hospitals in North Korea to treat and manage patient care. The Departments of Pediatric Rehabilitation Medicine and Chiropractic Specializations were also established. The Chiropractic Specialization Department provides life-changing treatment for patients through nonsurgical spine adjustment and joint and muscle treatment. The Pediatric Rehabilitation Department serves the needs of children with a variety of developmental disabilities, including cerebral palsy and autism.

On top of these medical advancements, special education for children with developmental disabilities was also established. Joy and I first coined the term "pediatric behavioral and developmental disorders" in North Korea to include not only cerebral palsy but also down syndrome, autism spectrum disorders, intellectual disability, and twenty-some other disorders included in developmental disabilities.

In 2015, with support from other organizations, the Department of Pediatric Rehabilitation Medicine opened not only in Pyongyang but also in three other provincial children's hospitals in North Korea. The Pyongyang Children's Hospital also added treatment for children with cerebral palsy after we began training doctors for the work.

Best of all, North Korea has begun to pay attention to these children. We are grateful that North Korea is making a national policy for underprivileged children and is actively trying to treat these children and incorporate them into society. Medical care is free in North Korea. There is no cost for examination, treatment, or surgery. This particularly benefits children with disabilities.

In the process of creating this system, it was Joy who gave me the most encouragement and strength. Before coming here, Joy worked as a high school science teacher in the United States. In Asia, she taught our children by herself. When our three children began attending the Pyongyang Korean School for Foreigners, she made use of her time by accompanying me to the hospital. Consequently, she began to use her skills, education, and calling to serve the children with disabilities in their educational needs.

Now one of the goals of treatment for children with cerebral palsy is to rehabilitate them enough so they can attend school. Education is essential for them to become an active member of society. While I was focused on their bodies, in Joy's eyes, this was the biggest need that she saw to help these children. So she set about finding a way to not just treat our patients but also educate them.

At that time, a new specialty in the United States was educational therapy. As an extension of special education, educational therapy goes beyond just making accommodations and modifications for children in the classroom. It individualizes education, thereby helping students overcome their disabilities. In other words, it simultaneously treats the disability while providing an education. The combination of treatment and education produces exponential results. For example, she provides strategies to help develop connections between the right and left hemispheres of the brain while teaching a child their numbers.

Though the internet is restricted for North Koreans, foreigners have access, and Joy started studying educational therapy day and night through online distance learning programs. After that, she became even more skilled in creating educational programs for children with behavioral and developmental disabilities.

Parents and teachers are no different in North Korea than anywhere else in the world. I met parents every day there who sacrificed much to give their children a better hope and a future and teachers who went above and beyond the transfer of information to help the next generation be a little better off. They had the same earnest expectations for their children. In these hidden places, they offered one another the love of God.

Neither Joy nor I were qualified to do what we were doing in North Korea. We only made ourselves available for God to do His work.

LOVE MEETS YOU WHERE YOU ARE

JOY AND STEPHEN

He made himself nothing by taking the very nature
of a servant, being made in human likeness.

—PHILIPPIANS 2:7

A number of changes occurred in the Rehabilitation Department a year after Olivia's drastic transformation. First of all, the number of patients that came to the hospital increased day by day. The more they came, the more we thought deeply about what we were doing. We started treating patients with cerebral palsy, but there were many other children that we could not help. Among them were children with autism. But we were not yet equipped to treat autism spectrum disorders (ASD), and we had no choice but to turn those patients away. Our team began to pray for God to send people with other medical specialties to treat children with various disabilities.

In the winter of 2015, a white American lady named Allyson approached us at a conference we were attending in Asia. She introduced herself as a therapist who had been working with autistic children and their parents in China for approximately twelve years. She felt that God was pouring a desire in her heart to serve children with autism in North Korea, and she began to pray.

While listening to her story, we shared with her about the many autistic children who came to our treatment room that we had to turn away because we had nothing to offer them. Allyson's eyes teared up hearing this, perhaps because she understood much better than we did the pain of an autistic child and their families.

Now, miraculously, it seemed God was sending us a therapist who could help these children. Three months later, Allyson visited Pyongyang. Her method of working with children who had autism was a treatment method called DIRFloortime® therapy. To put it simply, through this method, the therapist gets down to the level of the child, connects with the child at that level, and then challenges the child to develop further. This therapy does not force the child or require the child to do anything. The therapist simply enters the world of the child with autism and then waits for the child to respond. Sometimes the therapist has to wait until the child acknowledges that someone is by his or her side. When the child connects with the therapist, then the two of them begin to engage in play together, little by little. Through this process, the therapist enters the child's world and allows him or her to learn for themselves how to connect with people and build relationships with them. It's an incredibly Christlike way of serving these patients, and we saw Allyson engage with these children like Jesus again and again over the next two years she served with us on our team.

As news spread that the Pyongyang Medical School Hospital was now treating children with autism, parents began bringing their children to our treatment room. Leo's mother brought her nine-year-old son to the hospital. Like most children with autism, Leo had difficulty interacting with others, and he was our first official patient with ASD in Pyongyang.

At first, Leo's eyes were full of fear as Allyson approached Leo. He was playing alone, but she gently persuaded him to interact with her through sensory play. Over the span of a few days, Leo slowly began to make eye contact with Allyson. For a child who was not aware of the presence of other people and was confined to a world of his own, making eye contact with others was significant progress.

Leo had never had a conversation with his mother. His eyes had never properly met with hers, but as he connected with Allyson, Leo began to change. Allyson simply stayed next to Leo in close proximity. However, this child, who had never uttered a single word before, communicated with the therapist during that short treatment period of one week.

A few weeks later, Leo's mother told us an amazing story. At school, Leo approached another classmate who didn't bring a packed lunch and offered to share his own lunch with him.

Leo's teacher was shocked that Leo even approached another boy. Before therapy, this kind of interaction from Leo was unimaginable. Leo's mother was so touched that as she shared the story with us, she choked up, unable to finish her words.

Perhaps Leo really wanted to be friends with this child, but before treatment, he could not express it because he was locked in a neurological state caused by autism. When someone willingly entered Leo's world, though, and met him at his level, it opened a path to his heart that enabled him to care for others as well. More than someone teaching Leo this new skill, it was as if the resemblance of His Creator was being unleashed from within.

Through Leo, we began to see many possibilities to help these children. For two years, Pyongyang Medical School Hospital worked to learn about the symptoms and treatment methodologies for children with autism. This visiting therapist from the United States gave lectures and clinical training for four weeks in which more than thirty doctors from the Pyongyang Medical School Hospital and the Children's Hospital participated and hundreds of children's lives were impacted.

As we think about the challenges of unification in Korea and the many divisions in our world, churches, and homes, we realize we have so much to learn from the example of parents of disabled children and the therapists who work with them. These people show us what patient, accommodating love looks like. They show us how to approach those who are different with compassion.

It's love like Jesus has for us. Jesus met us in a state when we were disabled—turned inward on ourselves by sin—but he came down to our level and loved us so much he gave himself up to heal us, even while many still do not recognize him or understand who he was. He doesn't demand that we change on our own or force us to perform on his timeline. Instead, he accommodates us in our weakness. His love is what opens the door to our hearts and allows us to extend that same Christlike love to others.

So here's the challenge: let's love like Jesus. Let's be willing to get on the same level as those around us, even when it's uncomfortable. Let's enter into their world with patience, walking with them step by step toward healing. Whether it's in our families, our churches, or on the global stage, we can be the hands and feet of Jesus, breaking down walls and building bridges through his accommodating love.

And here's the amazing thing. As we extend that Christlike love to others, we may just find that it unlocks something powerful in us too. We grow in our capacity to give and receive love. We gain a deeper understanding of our shared brokenness and humanity. We get a clearer glimpse of God's upside-down kingdom at work in our midst.

WHEN THE
HARVEST IS HIDDEN

STEPHEN

*Let us not become weary of doing good, for at the
proper time we will reap a harvest if we do not give up.*

—GALATIANS 6:9

The day that Oliva left the hospital, after the farewell party
was over, I was left alone in the treatment room. The pediatrician on our medical team who helped on cases like Olivia's
opened the door and came in. She looked at me and suddenly
started to cry. Flustered, I quickly got up and placed my hand on
her shoulder.

"Why cry on a good day like today?" I asked. I wondered if something had happened.

With tears streaming down her face, she replied, "Doctor, what should I do? I never thought these children could ever be saved. So many children have come to my office, and I've told their parents to just let them go. I had no hope to offer them, so I told them it would be better not to let their children suffer any longer. Doctor, what if all of the children I sent away could have been helped? Those children . . ." She stopped speaking and choked with emotion and regret.

I put my hand on her shoulder as she cried. We actually cried together for some time. Watching Olivia regain function, I only ever dared to guess at what this doctor surely must have felt throughout this past year as she watched Olivia too. I had nothing else to say. Shaking her hand tightly, I assured her that from now on, one child at a time, we would somehow save more children.

There were times when we were in North Korea that I wanted to give up and run away from the life we'd made there. Sometimes the burden was too heavy to bear, the work too difficult to do. Often, when I woke up in the morning, I just wanted to pack my bags and leave.

Living in a cold house with frozen-over toilets, raising children in isolation, going to the market but not being able to buy what we wanted, and suffering from food poisoning during the hot summer months were not good motivating factors for us to stay. But despite these difficulties, deep down in my heart, I knew I could never really leave it behind. Honestly, the times that I really wanted to leave were when the work we were doing didn't show any results. At that time, I was about thirty-seven years old. I was in the prime of my life, but I often felt like there was no fruit for my efforts, for my pouring out all my energy for this land.

Is anything changing as a result of what we do? I ran around working day and night, but it felt like there was no tangible fruit that I could actually see. It seemed like I was wasting my precious time, my prime years. *Why am I doing this?* I often wondered. I had countless meetings, day after day.

Life in Pyongyang was not easy. Everything had to be done according to the rules, by the book. Everything was controlled. Stress was difficult to overcome. I was the only foreign resident doctor in the hospital, and this required that I be made to show the results of my medical treatment to the hospital executives. I was frantically busy trying to meet all their expectations. Our entire team was exhausted from managing the project and the construction of the hospital.

That night her confession cleared up all the confusion that was floating around in my mind about our work. It was a great comfort to me and the members of our team who had the weight of the world on our shoulders. It wasn't that there was no fruit from our work. This doctor confessing her acknowledgment of the value of one life was tremendous fruit from all our work. It was recognizing the value of a single person. To her, a child with a disability was no longer a burden to society but a life worth celebrating and sharing. This was the gift of life. Wasn't this the reason why our family came to North Korea?

At that moment, I came to understand. Christianity did not have to be explained in a grandiose way. As the scripture says,

"Whatever you did for one of the least of these brothers of mine, you did for me" (Matthew 25:40). We were just called to be with those who seemed small and hidden, those who were ignored and not given attention. It became clearer that this was our task in North Korea. Even if it seemed as though nothing was happening.

One day, when the stress of it all got to me to the point that I couldn't bear it anymore, I asked Joy if we could leave North Korea.

Instead of asking about what was happening, Joy turned to me and said, "Don't judge what you do based on what you can see. You need to focus on what we cannot see."

She was clearly much more mature than I was.

That night I remembered what my wife had said. My dear, godly wife must have foreseen this beautiful moment as a hidden treasure of faith. That doctor's confession caught my full attention. The admission and acknowledgment of this one person was reason enough for us to remain in North Korea.

There are times when it seems like there is no way forward, there is nothing to offer, and there is no way to know how things will turn out. When those times come, I will remember this doctor's confession. Even though we cannot see it now, we will dream of the things not yet seen, waiting for the wonderful mystery of God to be revealed.

Even if we do not reap any fruit, there is no need to be discouraged. I may sow the seed, and someone else may water it. But it is God who makes it grow. If one day someone reaps the harvest we have planted here, that is fine with me.

32

FINANCIAL SUPPORT ISN'T JUST ABOUT MONEY

STEPHEN

And my God will meet all your needs according to the riches of his glory in Christ Jesus.

—PHILIPPIANS 4:19

Our biggest concern when setting up a shoe company was finances since, at that time, we had no money to start a business. North Koreans must have wondered how we could do business in their country without a single penny to our name. The only thing I could trust in was God.

In April 2008, I was riding a van in China from Hunchun to Yanji, and a foreign man was sitting in the seat next to me. At first, I assumed that he was Russian, but then he introduced himself as B. T., a businessman from America. He was also on his way back from visiting Rason, North Korea. We started up a conversation, and I learned that he came to the region to help Christians engage in North Korea by creating opportunities through business. However, after his visit, he still had not found a suitable business.

Thinking of my father, I brought up the plan to establish a shoe-manufacturing company in North Korea. I explained that my father had close to thirty years of experience in the shoe export business. Hearing this, he said that if someone with ample business experience like my father could work in North Korea, then he thought that the business could surely be successful, and he was interested in becoming an investor in the company.

If that wasn't shocking enough, I was totally bewildered when he offered to make an initial $20,000 investment in the factory with no strings attached. He handed me his business card and asked me to contact him with a business proposal if we were interested in working with him.

As soon as I arrived in Yanji, I told my father and our team members what had happened. After deciding to take him up on his offer, we put our heads together to come up with a business plan. We thought that we should ask for $40,000 to start the shoe manufacturing company. After reading our plan, B. T. responded by saying that we were missing some key elements in the business, which would require a larger budget. We revised the business plan based on his advice and sent it back and forth multiple times. As we did, the initial necessary investment multiplied several times as well. We worried that the investment was becoming too large, but our investor continued to suggest more revisions. In the end, our original budget of $40,000 increased thirtyfold larger, to $1.2 million.

We were skeptical that this was going to turn out well.

But we shouldn't have been. We got every cent we needed of that $1 million, and this investor continued to help the business for another five years. His investment allowed our team to build a factory, reside in North Korea, and create jobs for over 120 North Koreans.

The more I think about it, the more miraculous it all was that my father agreed to move with us, that he had experience in the exact industry we needed to start a business in, and that I met a stranger on the van with the heart and resources to help us fund and build that business. When the two of us met that day in the van, God made both of our dreams come true.

God provided in similar amazing ways when it came time for our team to build a hospital. I was young and had already built a few kindergartens and rural clinics, so I thought building a hospital would be similar. Our hospital budget was around $200,000, and I wanted to do it right. So I asked a well-known Korean American architect to design a modern hospital building for us.

I was impressed with his design. Though it was designed with expensive taste, I took the blueprints into Pyongyang anyway to get an estimate for how much the building would cost. Surely, if a beautiful building like this was built there, it would be received with open arms, I thought. However, when a Chinese construction company determined the cost, they said that it would require approximately $1.5 million. I almost fainted.

We had sent Blessing back home because there was no sufficient inpatient room in the hospital, and that filled me with the desire to build a better ward for children with disabilities. Our objective was to build a good hospital where parents could care for their child with disabilities in special rooms. Comfortable hospital rooms and a hospitable environment can go a long way to encourage parents who go through so much. So the hospital design was revised, and the three-story building was expanded to six stories. We didn't have money for this. Nevertheless, the hospital plans continued to expand according to the needs around us.

Once again, the hospital project multiplied, and a $4 million project was born. We didn't even have the original $200,000, so how were we going to pull this off?

Because of the ever-worsening political situation, everyone told us that we should wait for the political situation to improve. But I was in a hurry. Children were losing their lives. We couldn't put off building the hospital any longer.

In 2014, when we were visiting the United States, a friend heard about what we were doing and suggested that we start raising funds. Our friends lived in the Silicon Valley in San Jose, and they helped host an event where we could raise funds for the hospital. About fifty people showed up, most of them second-generation Koreans with good jobs, but we only raised about $3,000.

Having high expectations, we were greatly disappointed.

At that time, a Christian acquaintance from China was in the San Francisco area and invited us to visit his family. He asked us if we would be willing to share about our work for ten minutes with their church's small group. Although this was a mainstream American church without much interest in North Korea, we used our time just to talk about our lives and work without any fancy multimedia presentation.

I briefly talked about treating children with cerebral palsy, and Joy shared her testimony of how our family was called to North Korea. After the meeting, one man came up to me and asked us what it was that we really needed. I never directly asked people for money, so I hesitated, not knowing exactly how to reply to his question.

After telling us to think about our answer, we were invited to his home the following day. Our friend encouraged us to be bold; this man could give us everything we needed.

Joy and I slept restlessly that night. How much money should you ask for from someone you don't even know? Should we tell him how much money we actually needed? Is it even guaranteed that we would be able to complete the hospital in Pyongyang?

When we went to his house the next day, we noted his home was nice enough to have a winery in it! It turned out that this man was a doctor and that he had developed a drug for an incurable disease. He told us that even if he spent money every day for the rest of his life, he would never run out because of the profits he got from his patent. Typically, he gave money to help individuals start new ministries, but that day, he explained, God gave him a heart to support our ministry in North Korea.

Hearing this, I openly shared with him our plan to build a hospital for children with disabilities and that all we needed to build it was money. He gave us $800,000 with one condition: it was a matching contribution.

"This work cannot be done by one person," he explained. "You need a lot of people praying together."

He would give his money as other supporters also gave for the project and then match their funds. So if someone gave $100, it would be doubled to $200. In this way, many people would be motivated to contribute to the hospital.

Following his promise, we began to raise funds, informing everyone that their donation would be doubled by a matching grant. As funding started to come in, with each donation, people prayed with sincerity for the construction of the hospital and our work.

When I look at the building today, I see it is a testimony to the work of God in hearts both inside North Korea and around the globe.

Many people think that doing work overseas just requires enough money. At first, I thought this too, and I really worried about it. Of course, some amount of financial support is a must, but now having worked in North Korea, I have realized that money is not the only necessary thing. God's interest is in people.

I have seen countless times that sufficient money is not what completes a project; God accomplishes what He wants to do through people.

SPECIAL GIFTS FOR OUR FAMILY

JOY

Let the little children come to me, and do not hinder them, for the kingdom of God belongs to such as these.

—MARK 10:14

While living in North Korea, God gave our family of five a very special gift: the blessing of another child through adoption. While treating children with disabilities, we added two more adorable children to our family through adoption, Jacob and Esther.

Whenever we met parents who brought their children with cerebral palsy to the hospital, it was hard for us to relate to them.

We contemplated how we could understand them better to help them more effectively.

One roadblock we encountered was not about medical treatment. Instead, convincing parents to allow their child to go through our program was one of the most difficult tasks. All the parents had hoped that if they brought their child in for treatment, their child would suddenly be healed and freed from all disability. However, pediatric behavioral and developmental disorders are rarely cured 100%. So treatment is primarily focused on minimizing disability while empowering them to overcome social obstacles so that the child can participate in daily life.

Treatment for these children takes a long time, and many will end up living their whole lives with at least some aspects of their condition. As a result, parents who want a quick fix often give up within just one month of treatment. No parent wants to give up hope for their child, but if there are no other choices available, the harsh reality of raising a child with a disability for life hits North Korean parents hard.

North Korea is a powerfully collectivistic society. Everyone has to work together and fulfill social expectations. In such a society, having to receive help from others your entire life creates a huge stigma. Parents of children with disabilities are largely concerned about the burden their children place upon the community. The harsh reality that your child may be confined to a wheelchair, only able to communicate through devices, and live like this for the rest of his or her life is extremely painful. Above all, parents want to prevent their child's pain from living in a society like this. It is another reason behind the position many take of allowing them to let their children go sooner rather than later.

Understanding their feelings, we persuaded these desperate parents to find some way for their child, even with a disability, to adapt within society. We also began to pray for our hearts to become more compassionate toward those parenting children with disabilities.

For many years, I had a desire to adopt a child. I had grown up with other families who had adopted children from Korea. When we started treating children with cerebral palsy, this thought came back into my mind. But my husband was afraid.

We already had three children, and raising children in North Korea was often overwhelming. However, his love for North Korean children and the heart of wanting to relate to the parents of his patients was so great that he decided to give adoption a try. Once the decision was made, we started to immediately look into adoption, only to find that in North Korea, foreigners are not permitted to adopt.

Our youngest biological daughter, Anna, started asking for a younger brother. Though we knew that we weren't going to have any more children of our own, we also knew that the possibility of adoption was impossible in North Korea, so I encouraged Anna to pray. She prayed for a little brother for six months straight at every meal.

Around January 2016, we attended a meeting in Thailand and happened to meet a family traveling on vacation who had twelve children. The parents were white, but most of their children were Asian. When we introduced ourselves, we found out that they had four of their own children but then had adopted eight Chinese kids. Besides that, six of their children had moderate to severe disabilities. We were shocked.

The mother introduced herself as a social worker who worked for an adoption agency specializing in children with special needs. After meeting her, we applied to become adoptive parents with the agency she worked for.

Shortly afterward, we received five pictures of children with cerebral palsy. Our family laid out all the pictures and prayed over each child. In the end, we decided which child should join our family forever. The child that was given to us at that time was Jacob. Jacob was found on the front steps of a hospital in China when he was approximately seven days old. He grew up in a facility for children with disabilities in Shaanxi, China. He was diagnosed with ataxic cerebral palsy and was registered with the adoption agency when he was two years old.

Anna's prayer had been answered!

As with having any child, a lot has changed in our home since Jacob joined us. More liveliness came into our family, and our surroundings became brighter. In particular, Jacob, who did not learn to walk until after three years of age, got stronger day by day as we provided therapy for him at home. Six months after joining our family, he was walking on his own with smooth, strong steps. We put all our heart and energy into helping Jacob improve.

Less than a year after adopting Jacob, our eldest daughter, Sarah, called us together saying that she had something to share with us after doing her morning devotions. God told her that our family should adopt one more child, she declared. She was convinced that that was what God wanted.

We thought that we had been obedient to God by adopting Jacob. Raising three children was like a war zone, and then we had Jacob too. Wasn't that enough? I had to spend a lot of my time focusing on Jacob with his special needs. My heart was for adoption, but the reality of it all was still quite burdensome. In the end, I was easily persuaded though, but it wasn't until Stephen gave us the go-ahead that we proceeded.

To be honest, despite the provision for the factory and the hospital, the main thing we worried about was how we would be able to afford this. Tears flowed down Stephen's cheeks every time he prayed about it. All we could do was obey in faith. The more we prayed and meditated on Scripture, the more we were convicted that it was the right thing to do. As we prayed, more love covered us, overcoming our fears.

While looking for what country to adopt from, the option of Georgia came up. Georgia is a small country that was once a part of the Soviet Union with a population of about 4 million. After receiving a few referrals, once again we received a picture of a possible child. I texted the picture to Stephen, who was away on a business trip. Strangely, this particular picture of a little girl from Georgia captured his heart. The moment he saw her picture, he knew that she would be our little daughter. Two-year-old Esther came to our family being born with congenital abnormalities. She had no calf on her right leg; rather, her foot was attached to her knee. Her eyes were severely crossed, and she had seven toes on her left foot. As soon as Esther's biological mother discovered her abnormalities after birth, Esther was sent to live in an orphanage.

Once we adopted Esther, we took her for an orthopedic evaluation. We decided to operate on her right leg and remove the two extra toes. By amputating her foot, she could be fitted with a prosthetic right leg. She also underwent surgery on both eyes. Although Esther may still need more surgery in the future, she is now seven years old and definitely improving little by little.

Although Jacob and Esther lived in orphanages for only two to three years, they had already experienced the trauma of abandonment. This was the biggest hurdle to overcome. As we parented them, we wanted to heal their emotional trauma just as the physical bodies of children with cerebral palsy were treated in the hospital. As new adoptive parents, we tried to overcome their trauma with love, even if that love came later in life. However, they often felt empty, not knowing how to receive that love.

All of a sudden, I wondered if God felt this way when He saw me. So many nights I spent in prayer and repentance. What I discovered while dealing with children who have disabilities and trauma is that there is inevitably a change, but that change happens slowly. And that slow pace is perfectly normal.

Above all, as a parent of a child with special needs, I saw myself frail and weak, and it was at that point that I realized how North Korean parents must feel. Despite the daily struggles, the next morning there can come a sense of thanksgiving for how far your child has come. This, I realized, is only possible through the power of love.

Raising five children is not easy, but these children have given us the greatest opportunity to discover our own weaknesses. Once again, we were humbled and grateful for the way that God always went before us. Children are a gift from God, and how many precious gifts we have received! Through adoption, we have learned the significance of a single life, both spiritually and personally, as we parent our children.

As parents came to the hospital for their children to be treated, I realized that it was not just about the children and their families but also about the doctors and our attitude while treating our patients. We were paving the road for these children. Even though progress was slow and it would take time, we would keep advocating. Children are precious. They are worthy of saving.

We want to go beyond the realm of treatment and education in North Korea. Our desire is to see society accept these individuals and adopt a new perception of disability. Just like seeing our own children, I want others to see the potential of one child. Each child has a purpose and a contribution to make to create a greater future for us all.

LIVING AS WORSHIPERS

STEPHEN

Be wise in the way you act toward outsiders;
make the most of every opportunity.

—COLOSSIANS 4:5

While we lived in Pyongyang, our family attended Bong-Su Church. Perhaps it surprises you to read that we publicly attended church at all. Believe it or not, the North Korean constitution states that there is freedom of religion in the country, and foreigners, in particular, are allowed to practice their religion. If you go into North Korea as a foreign Christian, you do have the right to practice your own individual faith, and many foreigners attend Bong-Su Church.

Because Christianity is one of the main religions of the United States, it tends to be rejected by North Koreans though. They hate Christianity primarily because it is viewed politically, not because they oppose it theologically. That is not to say there are no North Koreans in Sunday services though.

In order to attend church services, North Koreans must register their request with the government and be granted permission. Some in attendance had been granted permission, but we also understood that others in attendance might be assigned to be there to monitor the church activities.

Since Bong-Su Church is an officially state-sanctioned church, many claim that the church is just for show. We humbly confess that initially, we thought the same, but we began to experience God's grace and witness real worship while attending the church.

When the former senior pastor of the church passed away, a new pastor was appointed. From his lips, we heard the gospel proclaimed. It was Pentecost Sunday, and the message that day was especially inspiring.

"Let's pray that we all receive the Holy Spirit. May we keep our promise to be the Lord's witnesses till the end of the earth. Haven't all foreigners come here filled with the Holy Spirit to share His love with us? Let's go to our neighbors and do the same," said the pastor.

I didn't expect such a sermon while attending Bong-Su Church! Even if the church was established by the North Korean government, we believe that the Word of God is being proclaimed in this church and that God is working through it.

Didn't Paul also speak of this when he wrote about those who preached the gospel in an impure way? "Whether from false motives or true, Christ is preached. And because of this I rejoice" (Philippians 1:18). You may wonder how there could be God's grace in such a church. But in any church, whether large or small, do we not also experience the grace of God every week? If God gives grace, then we are to receive it. Every time the Word of God is preached, cultivating the soil of our hearts, then God is in the midst of it.

An elder who served in North Korea for many years told me that many of the independence fighters in Korea had been strong Christians, and their children are still serving in the North Korean government today. According to him, there were about 3,000 people in Pyongyang who identified themselves as having Christian heritage. He explained that those attending Bong-Su Church typically have registered with the government as possessing Christian lineage. Not just anyone can walk in and attend the church, only those who have explicit permission to do so. As a result, many congregants attend services because they want to be there, not because it's cultural or expected or routine, but because it matters to them to be there.

If what the elder said was true, most North Koreans at the church were rooted in some way or another to Christianity. As we attended week after week, we could see that most congregants sat in the same seat every Sunday. Some came early to read the church Bibles before the service began since they weren't allowed to take Bibles out of the church, but they could read them while in church.

After hearing this elder's explanation, I began to respect the North Koreans at Bong-Su Church, even if they were assigned to sit there by the government: God could still work in their lives too.

One Sunday morning, while I was sitting in the church, the Holy Spirit poured out unusual passion into my heart. It felt like God was taking special interest in me as He saw our family worshiping in Pyongyang.

Pyongyang in 1907 came to my mind.

At that time, the Spirit of God swept the world in an amazing way, and a great revival broke out in Pyongyang. The city of Pyongyang was known as the Jerusalem of the East because of the explosion of Christianity. Thousands of people came to Christ as they fell on their knees and repented of their sins. From the Pyongyang Revival, the church on the Korean Peninsula achieved tremendous growth. Even today North Korean officials acknowledge that Pyongyang was the epicenter of the Korean Christian movement.

We are worshipers on this land, a land drenched with prayers and tears. The Lord still loves this land and her people. He has not forsaken them. Our prayer is for North Korea to experience God again and rejoice in His presence, just as the pastor at Bong-Su Church preached. We desire for the glory of God to once again be fervently restored on both sides of the Korean Peninsula.

More than anything, this land is full of history, and I was saddened by the misunderstandings North Koreans have about Christianity. Since we cannot verbally preach here, the main way we are able to share God's love is through living by example, that is demonstrating Christ through our lives.

But we struggled with how well we were actually doing it.

One day, as we were leaving Sunday service at Bong-Su Church, an elderly Korean American from the United States started calling for me.

"Missionary Yoon! How are you?"

Most people know that they should not use the word *missionary* in North Korea. I was shocked! Why would this person say this out loud? Did he not know that this could lead to a lot of misunderstanding?

To North Koreans, using the term *missionary* connotes an imperialistic American with political objectives. There were North Koreans surrounding us, including North Korean officials, as he shouted to us from across the hallway. Joy and I were flustered and embarrassed as he blurted out this taboo word. We were puzzled as to why this person would act this way, especially while surrounded by North Koreans.

Our hearts sank.

The next morning, as I was heading out to work, our guide came to me and asked me not to go to the hospital that day. Instead, I was told we were going to take the day off and go for a walk. I followed along without knowing why, and our guide subsequently started to ask me questions.

"Why did you come to North Korea? Who is helping you?"

It was strange. I had already submitted all these answers in my letter to the officials when I first visited Pyongyang. They all knew the answers to these questions, but now they were asking me the same things again. I ended up not going to the hospital for several days. Every day I was taken to a different place and asked intense questions. It felt like I was being interrogated.

Then our guide finally looked at me and asked, "Mr. Yoon, I will ask you directly. Are you a missionary?"

At that point, I realized the seriousness of his questions. A lot of thoughts went through my head in that short moment. If I said something wrong, it could have drastic consequences. But at that moment, the Holy Spirit gave me inspiration. I realized that this was an opportunity to clear up misunderstandings about Christianity.

Instead of answering, I asked a question in return, "What is your understanding of the word *missionary*? Let's first see if we have the same definition."

The official's words became heated as he shared his definition of the word *missionary*.

"If you look at what missionaries did in the past," he explained, "did they not guide the army that killed our people during the colonial period?" He continued, "During the Korean War, Bibles were found on the remains of American soldiers. These Christians bombed and slaughtered innocent people. Isn't this the Christianity you are talking about?" Trembling, he went on, "Isn't this what missionaries do?"

His description of missionaries grieved my heart. Without knowing the true gospel of Christ, North Koreans saw Christianity intermixed with the colonial era and identified missions as the imposing imperialistic powers of the West. After hearing the official's explanation, I suddenly remembered the definition of *missions* that pastor and theologian John Piper spoke of in the book *Let the Nations Be Glad!*

John Piper stated, "The ultimate goal of the church is worship, not mission," and "The reason missions exist is because worship does not."[1]

I shared this with the official and said, "In Matthew 22, scriptures say that God came to the earth to show His love. Likewise, God has commanded us to love our neighbors."

---

[1]   Piper, John. Let the Nations Be Glad! Desiring God Foundation. 2022.

I wrote down John Piper's name and told the official to look him up and read for himself the definition of *missions*. I then explained further that our goal was to follow the missiological approach of this theologian.

"The missionary's ultimate goal is to restore worship where there is no worship. In this way, we can say that we are missionaries. Our purpose in coming to North Korea was to restore worship and to love God by loving our neighbors. That is our interpretation of the word *missionary*. We believe in God Almighty, and how He will bless this land as He is pleased with our worship. It is up to Him to bless North Korea, that is not something we can do. When our community said that we wanted to worship in Pyongyang, and our officials drove us to worship at Bong-Su Church, they allowed us to accomplish our mission in North Korea. When we worshiped in our hotel rooms and in our Pyongyang residence, we were accomplishing our mission. As Christians, our mission was to restore worship in North Korea."

Every word I said was written down by the official.

After a while, he came back and said, "Dr. Yoon, that is a very good definition of *missionary*. That is a good mission."

That evening the director of the department that was investigating me came to visit. He declared that there was nothing wrong with what we were doing and said that in the future, we would not have any difficulties because of the word *missionary*.

We were surprised by his words. Our family could have been in a much more dangerous situation, but thanks to God's protection and wisdom, this difficult situation gave us the opportunity to share the true meaning of missions.

We learned that part of our job was to break down the stereotypes of Christians and release North Koreans from their negative perceptions of Christianity. Perhaps that was even the main purpose of our being there, to resolve these misunderstandings about Christianity, paving the way for the gospel of peace. We wanted North Koreans to know that the God we believe in is not the political God that they had perceived. We hoped that the heart of Jesus would be demonstrated and shared with North Koreans.

Living as a Christian in North Korea or anywhere in the world means expressing the fragrance of Christ through our lives, not just in words. Our purpose on earth is to live as true worshipers where worship does not exist. For us, this means living a life of worship in North Korea. For you, it means living a life of worship right where you are too.

EARNING RESPECT
BY SHARING
THE STRUGGLE

JOY

We are therefore Christ's ambassadors, as though
God were making his appeal through us.

—2 CORINTHIANS 5:20

Back when we lived in Rason, I remember huddling together with our kids and our government guides to absorb the
small amount of heat from the space heater in the room to keep
our fingers and toes from freezing.

Every time a foreigner comes into North Korea, a guide is assigned to them. Our guides, or minders, went everywhere with

us at the beginning of our time in the country. If we were staying at a hotel, they slept at the hotel while we were visiting. Almost all our meals were eaten together as they were responsible for us for the entire time we were in North Korea. When we obtained residential visas or our own residence, our guides could go home in the evenings if they lived close by. Otherwise, they continued to stay in close proximity to where we lived.

For the first two years we lived in Pyongyang, our guide and driver actually lived in a back room in our residence. Later they moved to the building next door. We were not to go out of our hotel or housing complex without them. Usually, one or two people were assigned to you wherever you went. Although they were there to observe everything we did, they were also the people who solved many of our problems and became assistants to us and part of our administrative staff.

Sometimes we would stay with the same guide for one or two years. Once we started residing in North Korea long-term, we would work with the same guides for years. Regardless, North Korean guides who worked with our team had to work hard.

As we went about our work, our guides were right there with us. While traveling to the countryside to distribute food and medical supplies, there was a time when the van we were riding in got stuck in a frozen rice paddy. As the van crossed the frozen field, the ice cracked and collapsed, making it impossible for our vehicle to move. Each one of us, including our guides, got out of the car, gathered wood, and built a fire to melt the ice around our tires.

Another time, in Pyongyang, we had no running water for two weeks straight while the whole neighborhood was being re-piped. We survived on water being fetched from the Bo-tong River, which flowed adjacent to our residence. Our guides were right there with us during that as well.

As a result, we got close to our guides as if they were part of our family. One guide integrated himself so well with our family that he insisted on our kids calling him "uncle." He gave us a huge package of fresh crab every year for the holidays. Even though that guide has now gone on to other positions, some of the officials we worked with continue to be our closest friends.

I don't think the reason we were able to become close to our North Korean counterparts was because of what we did for North Korea. Instead, I think it was because there were times during our eleven-plus years of living together in which we suffered and endured hardships right alongside them. We worked together, side by side, in the thick of it. If at first they had suspicions about why we came to North Korea, I believe that as time passed, they probably only wondered why we didn't give up and leave when things got really hard.

When Stephen took a position as a professor at the Pyongyang Medical School, our family left Rason and moved to the capital city of Pyongyang. Life in Pyongyang was quite different from Rason. Much of it was unfamiliar, but we were able to overcome many difficulties because of the North Koreans in our community.

At first, we lived in an isolated compound on the west side of town. Guards patrolled the grounds twenty-four hours a day, and our only neighbors were high-ranking military officials whom we were not allowed to socialize with. We had no opportunity to socialize with other people. Our daily lives consisted of just hospital and home, living a completely isolated life. The only way we could leave our compound was by being accompanied by our guide. Our children had no friends to play with. We had no freedom at all. As a result, life for us was mentally challenging.

Our patience was stretched to the limit living in what felt like house arrest or indefinite quarantine for four long years. Unable to bear it much longer, we begged our guide to allow us to move to the foreign diplomatic compound on the east side of town in the Munsu District. If we could move there, our children attending school on the foreign diplomatic compound would then have the freedom to play with their friends. There were also shops and restaurants on the compound, which would allow us limited freedom to breathe! Our request was actually completely inappropriate since we did not have any diplomatic status, but it was the only solution we could think of that would allow us to keep living in North Korea. Our guide at that point had been with us for three years, and he sympathized with our isolation.

However, our guide came to us a few weeks later to let us know that our request to move was officially rejected, mainly because we did not have diplomatic status. Our hearts sank at the news. If we had to keep living in isolation like this, we would have to rethink our ministry in North Korea.

Then, all of a sudden, after two days, he came back to us saying that the approval had been granted and that we needed to quickly pack our things and move. We were puzzled about how this change of events had occurred, but we did what we were told nonetheless.

Later our guide's supervisor explained to us the reason for the reversal of the decision. On the day that we received our rejection, without our knowledge, our guide wrote a long letter

about us to his supervisor. He knew the hardships we had suffered while living in Pyongyang. Better than anyone, he was
someone who understood what we had gone through and how
much we loved North Koreans. He wrote a petition to appeal the
decision on our behalf, making sure that we could move to the
foreign diplomatic compound.

In fact, as US citizens, we had no right to make such a request because the United States does not have diplomatic relations with North Korea, and the foreign diplomatic compound
was primarily where diplomats lived. Regardless, the letter he
sent to his superior moved the hearts of the other officials, and
the decision was overturned. In this way, our family became
the first American family to ever live on the foreign diplomatic
compound in Pyongyang, and it was made possible only by our
guide. If he had not stepped out on a limb for us, we might either
still be living in isolation or have given up our work altogether.

I can't tell you how grateful we were. Life went from dull and
lonely to busy and social. We were able to walk freely to a store
on the compound and eat at one of the two restaurants there.
Our children could walk to school and even visit their friends or
have friends over at the house after school. After living isolated
for four years, we were finally part of a community again and
went to social events like movie nights, music performances,
and holiday celebrations.

We thought that because of all they had endured, North
Koreans would be hard-edged and tough. Like they would not
lose even a drop of blood if they were stabbed. As we lived life
alongside them, our stereotypes began to dissolve, and it was the
same for them as well.

It takes them a long time for them to learn to trust foreigners. But once a relationship is deeply established, they are willing to risk it all for their friends.

When people ask us how we've lived in North Korea and successfully negotiated through difficult circumstances, Stephen says half-jokingly, "All important decisions are made in the bathhouse."

But this is true. Public bathhouses are a huge part of Korean culture and society in both North and South Korea. In North Korea, bathhouses are even more important as private homes often do not have running hot water, so bathing at the bathhouse becomes both a necessity and a social event.

When you go into the bathhouse with North Koreans and sit naked, stripping yourself of everything but your common humanity, you begin to connect. You share your family's history and your life story. Both people come out knowing each other much better and connecting on a deeper level.

To the extent Stephen stripped himself down for them, he started to build trust little by little by removing preconceived notions. They jokingly said that when Stephen asked to go to the bathhouse together, they knew he meant business. There must be a problem to solve, they thought. But the truth is that trust built in the bathhouse is stronger than anything else.

Money cannot even buy it.

If you ask us how we gained the trust of North Koreans, we'll say it was simply by understanding their background and accepting their qualities as who they were. The more we deepened our understanding of the North Korean people, the more we had good results from working together. As we took little leaps of faith, each time we entered a deeper level within our relationship.

We had to adapt to some things living there, and they also had to adjust to us. As much as we had a hard time living as foreigners in North Korea, it must have been difficult for North Koreans to understand and accept our thoughts. There were many differences in worldviews and interpretations of events, but the fact that they accepted us to some extent demonstrated how much respect we had earned.

What was surprising was the fact that when we began treating each other within our community with respect, reaching out to each other with honor, the more we were able to win the North Koreans' hearts. We made a lot of mistakes, but looking back, it was IGNIS Community's ability to work through deep, trusting relationships with our North Korean counterparts that made all the difference.

North Koreans trusted us with important tasks, even though we had no money or specific expertise to back it up. We learned that North Koreans allowed us to do things because they chose to give tasks to people they could trust and to those who shared responsibility with them. This fact shattered our preconceived notions about them.

It is difficult to accept someone who comes from a drastically different background. However, it is necessary to accept each other's differences and develop a respectful attitude toward one another. Of course, this is true all around the world, not just in North Korea. Wouldn't polarization in our world start to lessen if we developed a sense of respect for one another?

Everyone needs respect. If you want to receive respect, you have to first give respect. Our own paradigms were transformed through this one word: *respect*. We need to be willing to let go of our pain and struggles in order to gain understanding and respect for others.

In the process of getting to know North Koreans, I also discovered who I was. Not all my preconceived ideas about North Korea were correct. As I grew to understand them, I also expanded my understanding of myself.

DIVISIONS AT HOME

JOY

He will wipe every tear from their eyes . . .
there will be no more death or mourning . . .

—REVELATION 21:4

It has been seventeen years since we first came to North Korea, but I sometimes still wonder what it means to live here. To me, living in North Korea is not about the number of years we've resided here but about sharing the major and mundane events of life with the people. We laughed together, cried together, and shared our pain and our joy together. It's been by living here that we've been able to build a stronger and more beautiful family, too.

People's initial reaction to our news of moving to North Korea was, "Why are you taking your children *there*?" It was an understandable reaction based on what most Americans think they know about North Korea. It seemed completely counterintuitive. Immigrants risk their very lives to make it to America in order to create a better future for their children, but it seemed like we were doing the opposite. Yet I firmly believed that our calling was not just for Stephen and me but included our entire family. There was no hesitation in that. But the reality of what it meant was more challenging to face.

When we arrived in North Korea, during winter, our children were six years, four years, and six months old. Our accommodation was a hotel right on the edge of the bay. From our window, we overlooked the port, and at night, we could see the lights from the fishing boats that were used to attract squid. Our entire team had to share one hotel suite, which consisted of three rooms with a narrow hallway between two of them. The hallway was used as a communal space where we set up our portable gas range and mini refrigerator. All heating was electric, and since there was little to no electricity in the winter, heating was scarce. Our hotel room was so cold that a glass of water would turn into ice overnight.

In order to sleep, we had to put on our stocking caps, gloves, and three to four pairs of socks. Each bedroom had multiple beds to accommodate as many people as it could at one time. But even so, it was so cold that by morning our entire family would be piled up sleeping in one bed all together. That was the only way we could maintain body heat. Watching our six-year-old daughter wake up with rosy cheeks from her skin being exposed to the cold air made us reconsider the reality of this calling on our children.

Occasionally, while traveling in South Korea or the United States, we would see the happy faces of other kids in Sunday school, and it would remind us of how isolated our own children were and how challenging the life we were called to was for them. Since we couldn't send our children to the government school, I homeschooled them all day in a cold room with almost no heating. In order to function, we had to wear thick, long underwear, which was lined with fake fur. Our kids wore fingerless gloves while doing their homework, but even while wearing hats and coats, we were shivering. Even when temperatures finally rose, there was no neighborhood playground to meet friends at and no Sunday school at our church. It was just us all day every day.

Sometimes we wanted to just run away to China where life was "normal." There they had reliable heat and internet. There we would have the freedom to move about as we pleased—to walk to the grocery store, visit shops, or play at an indoor playground. There we could meet more foreign families to make friends and fellowship with.

Once Stephen asked our eldest, Sarah, "Since it's so cold here, should we go back to China for the winter?"

But then Sarah smiled wide and confessed that she liked it here. That might have been because we no longer told her to change her clothes or take a bath. Since it was so cold, we rarely wanted to expose our skin to the air, and there was no hot water for baths anyway. To a six-year-old, that was happiness.

We had asked her because we wanted an out. We had wanted to use our children's needs and comfort as an excuse to run away from the work God had set before us. Putting your children first is a good thing; no one would blame us. But at the words of our innocent daughter, we couldn't help but give thanks because we knew it would be God's grace that sustained our family there. It's not only in the good times that we experience God's grace, but it is what gives us a heart of endurance when hardships linger.

While living in Rason, our children were constantly bored. There was no TV and hardly anywhere to go to play. Common North Koreans are not permitted to interact with foreigners, and if they do, they must report their conversation, in detail, to officials. Despite the frustration it caused them and the work it made for me, the boredom was actually a gift to each of us.

Every night the electricity was cut off after dinner, so we lit candles around our dining table, and the five of us would gather in the warm, yellow glow as the rest of the house sank into darkness with the setting sun. We spent every evening for about ten years together as a family, with no distractions from screens, friends, sports commitments, or extracurricular activities. With no other options, our kids talked with Stephen and me a lot, telling us their creative ideas for how to pass the time. We had time to read aloud Bible stories and stories of missionaries like David Livingstone, William Carey, Amy Carmichael, and Hudson Taylor. We spent a lot of time playing card games like Uno and Dutch Blitz. This extended quality time was an unforeseen gift from our choosing to live where we did.

We took our children with us as we traveled for our humanitarian work as much as possible. When we lived in Rason, we would take our children out into the countryside to rural clinics and kindergartens. They accompanied us when we made rice and medicine deliveries to remote clinics in farming and fishing villages. Since the mountain roads were so bumpy, the kids could not read or do homework in the car, but as soon as we had down-time at our destination, I would have our kids take out their books to do homeschooling in the car. When we moved to Pyongyang, our children would occasionally visit our treatment center and observe children with cerebral palsy receiving therapy.

When I asked our oldest daughter, now a college gradu-ate and public school teacher, about her childhood memories in North Korea, she said that she didn't want to forget any of them, especially the people. It was the people we lived life with there who made the biggest impact in her life. She looked at our North Korean guides as her uncles. She also called our driver "uncle." These North Korean "uncles" accepted our children as their nieces and nephews, and they'd shaped her life profound-ly. Because of our work, Sarah had the opportunity to shadow therapists at the hospital when she was in middle school. She attended lectures, along with North Korean doctors, on autism, and now she has decided to serve children with disabilities by pursuing a degree in special education.

We couldn't offer our children the best well-rounded educa-tion. We couldn't expose them to culture or even the "normal" things of childhood. All they could learn was what I was able to teach them. We read together, prayed together, and observed treatment at the hospital together. It was quite a unique educa-tional experience. But they also got to learn to embrace the North Koreans and how to love and pray for the people in their lives.

By living in North Korea, God also refined our sharp-edged marriage into a smooth pebble. Our marriage went through many rough waters while we lived in North Korea. Living under oppressive control, there was nothing we could do freely. We were watched every day, all day, and had tremendous stress on our shoulders because of that in addition to the work we were trying to do there.

I was the one who first received a calling for North Korea, but for many years, I could not participate much in ministry because I was taking care of and homeschooling our children. I was incredibly lonely. Not only did I feel like I was sidelined from the work I felt called to do, but I was completely isolated from other adults, with almost no one to talk to all day other than my children. I had no social life or freedom to meet people outside of our team, and weeks, sometimes months, would go by without having anyone to talk to in English apart from my family.

As the team leader, Stephen always had more work to do than time to do it. He had never-ending meetings, and no matter how hard he worked, where he went, or what he did, there was always something that wasn't getting done. Every time he needed to take a business trip, the kids and I would be left behind. We often would have to hold the fort down in North Korea while he was away in Europe, the United States, or elsewhere. Frustration, stress, spiritual oppression, and isolation drove both of us to tears many times. It's hard to explain how suffocating living under these conditions can feel.

A fierce spiritual battle was deployed to destroy our relationship. We were in North Korea to shoulder the burden and pain of the North Koreans, but we were falling short of shouldering each other's pain. The two of us would often fight only to end up not knowing what we were really fighting about. Sometimes there was no reason for fighting other than our exhaustion. After hours of lashing out back and forth, we would turn to each other and not even know why we were fighting. We could see that a spirit of division was trying to destroy our marriage. Satan attacks the family, which is the foundation of both the community and the church. If the family collapses, then everything else will suffer.

In order to stay there, we had to overcome this anguish caused not just by our personal frustration but by the complete social isolation and lack of spiritual support. Overcoming these obstacles was only possible when we realized that we were fighting a spiritual battle. Satan was attacking what was most precious to us, and that was our marriage and family. There were circumstances that we could not control because of living in North Korea. I had to give the situation over to God and submit to His plan. When I stopped trying to control and fix everything and instead relied more upon God and His strength for us, we found peace in our marriage regardless of the circumstances we were in.

One year we attended a conference in Switzerland for cross-cultural workers suffering from trauma. We met a woman serving in Iraq who woke up one morning and discovered that her roommate had been abducted by ISIS and decapitated. We could see that our situation was challenging but that others, like her, were serving in life-and-death situations. We realized we had much less to overcome by comparison, and that was a strange comfort to us. North Korea was actually more stable and safer than the challenges this woman faced, and we realized God had been merciful to us to call us to a place like this. But others attending the conference certainly looked at us the way we looked at this woman and wondered how we could live in a place like North Korea. But where God calls each of us, he also gives us the grace necessary to sustain us there. If you're following His call for your life, you're in the best and safest place for you to be, regardless of rulers or regimes.

As we shivered in the bitter cold when we arrived the first winter, the North Koreans would tell us to go to China and come back when it was warmer. But we endured it. We were cold with them. When they watched our suffering and struggles, they wondered why we didn't just leave. We didn't have to be there. Why were we staying there and living with them? When the North Koreans boldly asked us why we were living like this, we told them about the love of Christ. Christ taught us that he suffered for us. Our being with them in their suffering was a window into how Christ, our Immanuel, lived. It was by sharing in their suffering that we were taught the true meaning of love. We went there to live with them, to be with them, to love them.

After a few years there, while Stephen's father and Stephen were still running the shoe factory, people would bring the fish they had caught and give it to Stephen's father to celebrate the holidays. When they learned that he was suffering from diabetes, they would bring him brown rice, which was almost unheard of in North Korea.

"Father Yoon is also our father, so we have to take good care of him," they would say. "You have taken good care of us, so we will take good care of you."

This time, when we cried, it was not from hardship but from joy and gratitude because we had been accepted into their community as their fellow neighbors and from what God was able to do in our family and our marriage in these challenging circumstances.

WHY AM I HERE, LORD?

JOY

So whether you eat or drink or whatever
you do, do it all for the glory of God.

—1 CORINTHIANS 10:31

I had been wanting to live in North Korea since I was a teenager, and in the waiting season, God developed in me a passionate heart for this land. Even when we were afraid and struggling with the realities of life here, I held on to the clear direction of God's calling. Because of this clarity, it gave me hope, which enabled me to endure in obedience. Imagine my confusion when the reality of the ministry I felt called to left me sidelined and isolated at home, in a team where most leadership roles were given to Stephen.

It seemed there was not much that I could do to participate in the work and fulfill my calling, from home. I went through a deep valley of disappointment and isolation as I waited alone at home. As days at home extended to months, then lengthened to years, I questioned my purpose for being here. God had called me to live in North Korea, and I had come all the way here in obedience to His calling. I was extremely lonely and felt trapped between the life I felt called to and what life actually looked like. Although I was full of enthusiasm for the work our team was doing, I was at home, unable to participate in it. Being immersed in the disappointment of my reality, I walked through a dark valley of tears.

Other ministry and missionary couples have had similar experiences, but you needn't be in ministry to experience the fiction that comes in the space between what you expected your calling to look like and the reality of it. At this point of tension, I know I'm not the only person who has questioned my purpose and the meaning of my waiting and my suffering.

Then, just when our ministry took off in earnest, I was diagnosed with stage-three kidney cancer.

Why this too, Lord?

But God was watching over us, and He was the one providing for us and rescuing us in the midst of these difficulties. Even though I felt like I had contributed nothing besides showing up to His calling upon my life, God was still with me.

As we hurriedly left for South Korea to obtain a clearer medical diagnosis, leaving the kids behind with teammates, we were worried that it was already too late to get treatment. We worried if I'd be able to schedule surgery since it was Christmastime.

Thanks to divine connections, we were put on the schedule of one of the best surgeons in a hospital in Seoul, who declared, "I guess I left my Christmas schedule open for you."

I had my operation on Christmas Eve.

I began to understand how much the Lord is more interested in who we are—that is, how much we love Him, than in what we do for Him. What God wants is for us to fall deeply in love with Him, not just for us to strive for achievements through our work.

After a few months of post-op recovery, we returned to North Korea. The reality of my situation had not changed much. For the most part, I was still not able to be involved in ministry. But if there was one thing that changed, it was myself. Now, even if I could not be involved with what was happening, I was content to be in North Korea because that was the place where God had called me to. Even though I had no significant contribution to the work on the ground, I was able to worship Him, and that was enough. The greatest ministry is a life of prayer and worship, giving my heart and my desires over to the Lord.

As I was learning these lessons through my journey, I wrote a poem.

Why am I here?
Why am I here, Lord,
In a place where I don't belong,
In a foreign land with foreign languages and
foreign customs,
Among people who are so hard to reach,
Without a connection in the world,
Alone, so utterly alone?

What is my calling?

What is it that You have gifted me with?

I am so incapable,

Shrinking in my weaknesses,

Overwhelmed by my inabilities,

Without a role or purpose.

Yet YOU are here, Lord.

And You have called me here.

I may not be the best worker

Or servant

Or even effective in anything that I do.

Yet I am here for You, Lord.

You may not need me.

You may not even use me.

But receive my imperfect service all the same,

Help me to love You more,

Fill me with Your love,

So that others will receive Your love through me.|

Why am I here?

It is not for work or fame.

It is not because I am the best suited or gifted.

It is not for the effectiveness of ministry

Or for accomplishment of goals.

I am here for You, Lord.

For You and You alone.

My loneliness was turned into a prayer, and through communion with the Lord, I was able to confirm once again why we were here: to love this land and her people. I realized that my ministry in this season was not a ministry of "doing" but rather a ministry of "being." God called me just to be in that land, and our presence in North Korea and obedience to God was a ministry in itself.

In the "being," I was prepared for the "doing" that was to come. After waiting many years, I too had a special role in our work in North Korea. It was a job that was tailored to my education, experience, and interests perfectly—divinely designed for me. I became in charge of educational therapy in the hospital for North Korean children with cerebral palsy and autism, and I got to help pave a new path that was being paved in the North Korean medical community.

Stephen and I had held hands on this windy, wilderness journey. Both of us knew the answer to my question: "Why am I here?"

Our family had made it that far because we were convicted by the answer. We were there for the Lord, and we were there for those He loves.

LIVING
INCARNATIONALLY

STEPHEN

See, I am doing a new thing! Now it springs up;
do you not perceive it? I am making a way in the
wilderness and streams in the wasteland.

—ISAIAH 43:19

When we first started working in North Korea, there were no cell phones in the country, and there were few places in Rason where we could make an international phone call. Only a few official phone lines in the city had the ability to make international phone calls, and our hotel lobby had one of those phones. You could only make international calls if you had permission, and they were placed by the phone operators in the hotel's office in the lobby.

One day I went to the phone operator in our hotel to place a call to China. I was dressed like a typical North Korean man, in a navy-blue Mao suit, and told the operator in the local dialect that I needed to make an international phone call for work.

She curtly replied, "No!"

I had been making international calls back and forth for quite a while, so I found it odd and irritating that suddenly I was refused permission to call. I passed my identification to her and glanced at my guides standing behind me for help. They were watching the whole thing and burst into laughter when they realized that the operator had mistaken me for a North Korean and that was why she refused to allow me to make an international call.

Being mistaken for a North Korean could cause this kind of inconvenience, but it also meant that I had made inroads into assimilating into the culture enough to be mistaken for a native.

While living there, we had always dressed like North Koreans and worked to learn their culture. It was certainly easier for me to blend in here than Joy, but for both of us, the more we embodied their experience and understood them, the closer we got to them. We started to gain their trust more and develop friendships, and the more we did, the more we were able to accomplish without unnecessary conflict. We were given opportunities to share about who we were and what we were doing here.

It was important for us to maintain our faith and not feed into the propaganda that foreigners were bad people who should be seen as suspicious or who wanted to bring revolution or capitalism to North Korea. By embodying many of their cultural norms, it meant that we could live out our lives there as Christians and be accepted.

Everyone's thoughts are shaped by their experience, environment, culture, and community. Our life experiences were vastly different than most North Koreans', and we inevitably acted from a very different worldview than they had. While we could speak their language, we often did not share the same cultural perspective, so much of what we said seemed strange to the North Koreans.

The most important thing we had to begin to remember was that North Koreans think of their community and their country before themselves. For example, the whole country gathers in small groups every Saturday morning to receive education on current issues. This reinforces the unity of both purpose and thought. For those from the West, where individualism and freedom are highly prized, it's very difficult to understand how communal societies like this work.

Often, when I would treat patients, I gave them specific instructions as to what the patient should or should not do. At our next appointment, the patient would have often not followed my instructions and made no progress. The reason was that the things I had instructed them to do did not fit the community-first mindset of North Korean life. Though they knew that if they did what I said, they would get better, they wouldn't do it because it felt to them that their doing these things would come at the expense of their community. It felt selfish or indulgent to them to focus on their own needs, even if their need was healing.

So I began to teach my patients that their caring for themselves would make the community and society better and stronger. Only when I changed the way I prescribed did my patients start accepting my instructions.

It is not effective to approach issues in North Korea with an individualistic mindset. The issue has to be addressed in the interest of the group. As a result, Christians in North Korea have a reputation for being selfish and self-centered, because we often come from more individualistic cultures.

Just as Paul approached the Jews in the form of a Jew, as a weak man to the weak, and not as a free man but a slave in order to win all people, I was also challenged to approach North Koreans as a North Korean with a communal mindset so they could understand my intentions.

Christ too came in the same way, humbling himself and becoming flesh so that all mankind might know his love. It was this love that Christ gave us in human form, who walked among us and lived with us so that we might understand how great his love is for us.

"Your attitude should be the same as that of Christ Jesus: Who, being in very nature God, did not consider equality with God something to be grasped, but made himself nothing, taking the very nature of a servant, being made in human likeness. And being found in appearance as a man, he humbled himself and became obedient to death—even death on a cross" (Philippians 2:5–8).

Just as the Lord loved us and lived among us, so I want to live with the people of North Korea in order to share His love with them. For me, that looks like dealing with the interruptions of being mistaken for a North Korean and putting on their mindset in order to show them what is true in a way that they can take hold of it.

While there is no official church activity in North Korea, many Christians are there living out their faith through who they are, how they live, and how they conduct their work or run their businesses. Living there as a foreigner comes at a cost to personal freedom. Foreigners cannot rent just any apartment or house; they must live in specified compounds, hotels, or facilities. Internet access is not available in most areas, and international phone calls are limited and very expensive. Visas to foreigners are only issued for short periods, and because of that, individuals have to frequently go in and out of the country. Even after residential visas are obtained, most foreigners have to be accompanied at all times by official guides.

But by laying aside our worldviews and preferences and becoming like North Koreans, we are able to bring with us the presence of the Lord to this land. Just as Jesus incarnated, we must also incarnate into the lives of those we came to serve and become his hands and feet. When that happens, others are able to taste and see for themselves that God is good.

OUR TASK OF RECONCILIATION

STEPHEN

Therefore, if anyone is in Christ, the new creation has come. The old has gone, the new is here!

—2 CORINTHIANS 5:17

One day, while meditating on the book of 2 Corinthians, I suddenly felt like God was giving us a message for our ministry. "Therefore, if anyone is in Christ, he is a new creation; the old has gone, the new has come" (2 Corinthians 5:17). This means that as Christians, we should look at the world with new, redeemed eyes. We cannot be content with human thoughts and paradigms but must be stretched beyond the norms and into new horizons.

On the Korean Peninsula, North and South Korea have been frozen in a perpetual state of war since 1950. Although an Armistice Agreement was signed on July 27, 1953, a peace treaty has never officially ended the Korean War.

Before peace can happen, reconciliation is needed—not reconciliation of the conflicts between democracy and communism, capitalism and socialism, but the conflict in men's souls. True reconciliation is only possible when we have a new identity—that is, when we become a new creation in Christ Jesus.

The mission of Christianity is not to change the regime in North Korea, but to share God's love with the people of North Korea. I have seen many North Koreans reject Christianity for fear of the political leanings that often are brought with it in an attempt to change the country.

Some still have many negative thoughts about North Korea because of what the regime connotes, and these thoughts are a stumbling block to unity. The scars left by the Cold War are deep and long-lasting, and they exist even in the global church. I was quite shocked when I heard Christians call me a "red communist" because I was a humanitarian worker in North Korea. It made me question my identity.

At that time, God gave me a word that would enable me to stand before the church and individual Christians. That word was *reconciliation*. As I read the book of Corinthians, I came to understand this message even more clearly. God has indeed given us the ministry of reconciliation and called us all to be ambassadors of reconciliation. "That God was reconciling the world to himself in Christ, not counting men's sins against them. And he has committed to us the message of reconciliation" (2 Corinthians 5:19).

When I was called to North Korea, my prayer became how to bear the pain of the church while also treating the people of North Korea. This tension was a constant struggle. As a result, our community began to focus on reconciliation. As believers, the only way to restore people who are in conflict, separated from and hostile toward each other, is through reconciliation.

Is this not the realization of the kingdom of God that Jesus spoke about in the Sermon on the Mount? Just as the Lord taught us how to pray, "Forgive us our sins, as we also forgive those who sin against us," so we are to pray for God's kingdom to come here on this earth.

The kingdom of God is not any worldly governmental system, neither democracy nor communism. God's kingdom is where there is reconciliation between me and God, and between me and others around me. It is only when we ourselves are reconciled to one another that the world around us can be healed from our long-festered suppressed hurt and wounds.

Nothing happens in an instant. Likewise, reconciliation must be put into practice. Those who really desire reconciliation, we must start within. This means overcoming generational drifts within our own families, reaching out to those different from ourselves, and healing division within our own churches. We cannot blame one another—that is, we cannot blame the conservatives, the liberals, the progressives, or any person or faction for the impossibility of reconciling conflicts. If we cannot practice reconciliation in our mundane lives, then we have no right to talk about God's ministry of reconciliation.

Reconciliation first starts with me.

Ruptures in relationships, whether hatred and unforgiveness from interpersonal conflicts or lingering scars of war, are often found in the hearts of believers. It is not easy to talk about reconciliation because the context for it is often a tangled mess, and it can be hard knowing where to start. But it must start.

If reconciliation and unity cannot be achieved among believers, then how can we speak of reconciliation and unity with those so different and opposite to us? If the Lord's new commandment to love one another is not lived out and practiced in the church, then we cannot talk about Jesus's love flowing out into other parts of society. If love does not flow into society through the church, then how much hope do we actually have for Christ-centered unity?

In the book of Corinthians, Paul describes how much we, as the church, are to love one another. As members of the same church, we are all on the same level—that is, there is no master and no servant. Jews and Gentiles are both alike. The world is watching when churches fight. Therefore it is important that the church knows how to overcome conflict. I earnestly hope that the church will step forward in wrestling out their witness to the world. If Christians who have already experienced reconciliation with God cannot proclaim this message of reconciliation, then who can?

We are ambassadors for Christ. It is the role of an ambassador to convey the message of their host country or land, building a bridge between two different groups of people. God wants to heal the wounds of North Korea and every person and people group. He longs for reconciliation. For this, we, as believers, must take the first step forward. But in order to do this, we need to honestly ask ourselves, "Do we have a heart to mourn over this conflict?" and "Are we willing to lay everything down in order to get to know the other person?"

The message of Christ's reconciliation with us is our hope. Our calling for North Korea is not only to bind up the wounded nation but also to prepare the church and the entire world for the coming of the Lord. My personal hope is that reconciliation is not achieved just politically but, more importantly, accomplished interpersonally. Reconciliation starts first in the dark valley of relationships in the church. When we live out reconciliation in our own families, churches, and communities, then it may be possible to overcome our differences and bring unity cross-culturally.

I believe that the Lord will be pleased with us and give us the gift of unity when we live it out right here and now where we are at today. We must start reaching out to the people in our daily lives to begin the process of reconciliation. Now is the time to throw away the old wineskins. It is time to use the new skins to become a new creation in Christ.

SEEING NORTH KOREA
THROUGH GOD'S EYES

JOY AND STEPHEN

*Do not conform to the pattern of this world, but
be transformed by the renewing of your mind.*

—ROMANS 12:2

Peaple often ask us if it is hard to live in North Korea. "Extremely," is the honest answer. But despite the difficulties we faced, we are grateful for the privilege of serving the most vulnerable children in that country—children who were hidden and forsaken by the world, but not by God. He never forgot them and sent us to serve them.

As we followed the heart of God in serving the least of these, we came to know His love for them and for ourselves more fully.

North Korea has always been a land of controversy. International media focuses on North Korea's human rights issues, nuclear weapons, and economic hardships. While these issues are real and important, we must ask ourselves, *Is that all there is to the country?* Throughout our time there, God kept challenging us to learn to see North Korea through His eyes.

When it comes to North Korea, we tend to focus solely on the darkness. However, as believers, we are called to look at what God is doing in the midst of the darkness. When our gaze is fixed on the negative, we are focused on what Satan has done, not what God is doing. Like Moses sending twelve scouts into the Promised Land, we have a choice in how we view the challenges before us. Ten of the scouts were overwhelmed by the strong fortresses and giant inhabitants they saw, and they despaired for their future. Only Joshua and Caleb trusted that God would do what He said He would. Today we need the faith of Joshua and Caleb.

While living and working in North Korea, we had the opportunity to see her people up close, to witness those living in hidden places behind the politics and news. We met kindergarten children and their teachers, women who sewed for us in our shoe factory, hospital doctors, Blessing, and other children with cerebral palsy. It was evident that God was not giving up on these people.

It's important to understand that none of this was due to our great faith or because we possessed something special. It was God alone who taught us that His heart for His creation is not constrained by political borders or geographic boundaries. His love extends to the ends of the earth.

To us, North Korea is no longer a dark and unreachable land. God is present and active there, just as He is in South Korea, Illinois, or California. "For where two or three are gathered in Christ's name, He is in the midst of them" (Matthew 18:20). When we look at North Korea through God's eyes, we see a God who makes all things possible. His love has the power to heal nations— all nations—that are sick with the effects of sin and brokenness.

In the book of Revelation, John writes his vision of the New Jerusalem. There he sees "the river of the water of life, as clear as crystal, flowing from the throne of God and of the Lamb down the middle of the great street of the city. On each side of the river stood the tree of life, bearing twelve crops of fruit, yielding its fruit every month. And the leaves of the tree are for the healing of the nations" (Revelation 22:1–2).

As we work in North Korea, we get to see small glimpses of this heavenly promise fulfilled. When we do, we see North Korea through God's eyes—restored, reconciled, and her people revived. This is the hope we cling to as we continue to serve and love the people of North Korea, trusting in the transformative power of God's love to bring healing and redemption to what we think is the darkest of places.

Thank you for traveling with us on our own journey of learning how to love in North Korea. Because of our time in this nation, we will never be the same, and we pray that you have also encountered God's heart for His people and the world through this journey. Whether it be through working with chil- dren who have disabilities or ministering in reconciliation on the Korean Peninsula, we see our Father first pouring out His heart of lament and then compassion, mercy, and love. God meets us where we are, which means that God meets us in our brokenness, our pain, and our vulnerability. In that place, He stretches us to expand our definition of love. God is so gracious that He doesn't keep us in our own thoughts and ways. He breaks us down to rebuild us in a more holistic and restorative way, and He both teaches and shows us His unconditional forgiveness, mercy, and above all, love.

God is calling us each to His ministry of reconciliation. We do not have to go out of our way to find the broken, hurting places in our world. They are all around us. Whether it be the poverty in our inner cities; those on the fringe, outcast and discriminated against; or conflicts within our own neighborhoods, churches, and even families—God is calling us each to be ambassadors of reconciliation.

As the two of us have experienced in North Korea, God's healing power manifests itself in the rifts and shambles. His light shines brightest in the dark. In this way, God is calling us to embrace one another in His generous, unconditional love.

The Reconciliation Cross represents the heart of what the cross of Jesus Christ means for Christians. As we are reconciled to him, we are able to reach out our arms to those around us in love. The cross was designed by Young-in Choi and crafted by Pastor Seong-hwan Kim. To see more of his work, please visit **https://www.canacreation.com/**.

SUPPORT THE
IGNIS COMMUNITY

I GNIS Community is an International NGO passionately dedicated to nurturing the healthy development of children through vital medical and educational support. Unaffiliated with any government financial aid, we are sustained by the heartfelt generosity of individuals and businesses whose contributions make a profound difference where it is most needed. Your monthly donation of $20 transforms into a lifeline of essential resources like rice, medicine, and winter heating for children with developmental disabilities, their families, and other young children in dire need. Will you join us in our mission to light up the lives of these children in North Korea? We eagerly await your support and partnership. Together, small acts of sharing can ignite new hope and breathe life into countless lives.

ACKNOWLEDGMENTS

We are indebted to our IGNIS Community team members, our personal supporters, and IGNIS' many financial supporters, including supporting churches and individuals; our prayer partners; IGNIS board members; and all our mentors, colleagues, and partners who have enabled us to do what we do. They are too numerous to list, but we are thankful for each and every one of you. Without IGNIS Community, we would not have these stories to share. It has truly been a team effort, and only thanks to this teamwork can we testify to what God is doing in North Korea. We also want to thank our parents, siblings, children, and all our extended family members who have faithfully lavished their love and support on us throughout this journey. They have sacrificed greatly in many ways in the process, for which we are truly grateful. Above all, we thank God for the honor of being witnesses to His love and ambassadors of His reconciliation in the midst of conflict, misunderstanding, and pain. May His light shine bright in the darkness, and may He receive all the glory and praise!

ABOUT THE AUTHORS

For the past seventeen years, Stephen and Joy have served as Christian humanitarian workers to the people of North Korea and have lived in the country for eleven of those years. Together, they founded a nonprofit organization in 2008 known as IGNIS Community. Their cross-cultural work in North Korea has included humanitarian outreach, social entrepreneurships, and medical treatment and education.

Since the US State Department imposed new travel restrictions to North Korea, the Yoon family (including five children) has continued to serve children with disabilities throughout East Asia training parents raising children with disabilities and developing medical graduate programs in pediatric rehabilitation. Stephen still treats patients and trains doctors in these specialties, while Joy instructs in and oversees the special education and educational therapy programs.

As soon as the DPRK borders reopen, Stephen and Joy plan to return to full-time work in Pyongyang. Both are published authors, and their work has been featured in *Discovering Joy: Ten Years in North Korea*, as well as in various other publications, including *TIME* and *The Wall Street Journal*. You can learn more about the Yoons and their work at joyellenyoon.com or at IGNIScommunity.org.

To Learn More About the Yoons, Visit:

WWW.JOYELLENYOON.COM

www.ingramcontent.com/pod-product-compliance
Lightning Source LLC
Chambersburg PA
CBHW070919120626
46546CB00001B/332